Man Decoding Single Loving Woman

Romantic Perspectives

Part 1

A guide on women from a man's perspective

Nixon Mandigo

Acknowledgements

Many great thanks go to many people that made this book possible to publish. If their commitment had not shined through, the book would not be in existence. The success I achieved to publish this book shows that the contributions of these great individuals to the research over a long period were unflinching and selflessly given with the desire to contribute to a better world. My gratitude also goes to Ben and Nixon jr for employing their expertise towards the final part of publishing the book. I included a list of bibliography in acknowledgement of some ideas that shaped my critical thinking towards arguments that a presented in this book. I also want to give credit to my parents, partner, teachers and everyone that enriched my life by educating me about the meaning of love and the value of a vibrant society. Above all, I want to appreciate the exposure I gained from my clients. Most of my clients have no idea that they taught me the importance of cherishing diversity. As a result, my wisdom continues to get better with the information I receive from a diverse group of people.

Table of Contents

ACKNOWLEDGEMENTS 5

CHAPTER 1 8

CHAPTER 2 10

ASPIRATIONAL PHASE 10

   Personality Identifier Metrics 12

   Accepting Reality 14

   Comment 25

CHAPTER 3 27

SPOTTING PHASE 27

CHAPTER 4 35

INTERNET CHARACTERISTICS 35

CHAPTER 5 43

APPROACHING PHASE 43

   Techniques 51

CHAPTER 6 55

DATING PHASE 55

   Cluster Dynamic Metrics 59

CHAPTER 7 73

DOMINANT CLUSTERS 1 73

CHAPTER 8 87

DOMINANT CLUSTERS 2 87

CHAPTER 9 ....**100**

IMPACTFUL FACTORS...100

CHAPTER 10 ....**108**

PROPOSING PHASE 108

Compromising Theory.. *111*

BIBLIOGRAPHY **122**

Chapter 1

The book, 'Decoding the love woman', was written to educate the authentic man about the best qualities of a 'Love Woman'. The explanation contained is specifically targeted at men that love an everlasting and fulfilling romantic experience with a woman. The book helps a responsible man to understand and cherish the nurturing characteristics of women. The literature will develop men's understanding and appreciation of qualities radiated by women. Ultimately, the men will improve in the manner they evaluate, treat and accommodate women's expectations.

Consequently, the man would become realistic about his role in developing positive traits to achieve the best romantic experience. Equally, in reading this book, women would benefit from learning men's perception of them. Furthermore, women would identify issues they could help their men to improve in meeting their expectations. A woman will realise that she has a duty to provide intimate information to support a man in an effort to achieve a satisfying relationship. The book unlocks the essence of security, peace, confidence, respect and support to enjoy immensurable benefits of love with a female. It seems hard for most men to fathom the power of strong mentality and knowledge in shaping behaviour to achieve his dreams. Hence, the book is the best assert for men intending to live the best and everlasting experience of love and respect.

The paperback is written from a multi-dimensional perspective for men to eliminate the impression that all women are exactly the same. However, the book provides solutions that represent the best moral interests of various perspectives inspired in different societies. Notably, the book contains a framework that helps men to determine and evaluate their dominant characteristics. After a man understands his dominant characteristics, he would become confident to define his aspirations for meeting and loving a befitting woman. One concept in the book helps a man to describe the type of a woman that would be compatible with his personality. Similarly, the book reveals another concept that helps men to understand women's most preferred characteristics of the opposite sex.

If men could understand the women's ambitions, it would give them a chance to improve on their weaknesses. More so, if men knew the desires of women, they would know what to improve and confidently use to impress their dream women. As such, the concept gives a man an opportunity to evaluate and continuously improve characteristics that women generally crave. If men would be honest when evaluating their characteristics using the frameworks, they would deduce a realistic view of themselves. As such, this first book is a part 1 of the series that provide advice to men to strive for serious, loving, everlasting and respectful relationships with appropriate women. The part 1 book is suitable for men that aspire to achieve the best during the prospecting and dating journeys of their lives. Readers would benefit from the book if they understand the 'aspirational phase' that helps them to be successful in prospecting, dating and beyond.

Chapter 2

Aspirational Phase

Every man goes through an 'Aspirational Phase' where he defines the type of a woman he wishes to devote his entire love for 'eternity'. Lads that understand their personalities enjoy the best analytical experience during the 'Aspirational Phase'. It is reported that there are very few men that are capable of precisely defining their personalities in relation to love. As a result, men that were asked admitted that they had an inability to identify personality elements. They further professed confusion when undertaking an analysis process without proper guidance. The men stated that their methods of analysing the personality traits related to love were haphazard. They further expressed that the unsuitable and ineffective methods lead them into distressful relationships.

Consequently, the majority of men are not confident about the manner they project their personalities to relate and attract the right women. Therefore, men need help to identify elements that define their personalities. It is imperative for men to eliminate confusion and an inability to relate and attract appropriate women. Accordingly, a fella should be effective at evaluating his personality elements so that he understands his strengths and weaknesses. If the lad does not understand his personality elements, he would never be aware of the adjustments to make to become relatable to the right female. A man's idea would become clearer after identifying relatable personality elements that might converge with the most suitable female. If a bloke could define his characteristics, he would know the traits to emphasis or improve to achieve compatibility with a specific lady. The gentleman would also learn from using the analysis if there is a chance of discovering wide personality differences. As such, the male would develop confidence to define and implement strategies that allow him to find and convince a suitable woman that he is the right man for her. The fellow would effortlessly approach a suitable lady with confidence and charisma. Mostly, when a guy is confident about his abilities, he would find it easy to speak and express his feelings more fluently to a woman.

Ordinarily, persons that are involved in a romantic relationship can achieve fulfilment and everlasting success if they properly adjust their personality traits to become compatible. The frameworks in this book are essential for men to learn and develop effective skills on reading and adjusting personality traits to improve compatibility. If a fellow attains compatibility through making adjustments in some personality elements, he needs to consciously and tirelessly sustain the desired traits for the life of the relationship. A man can predict that his effort to adjust for purposes of maintaining compatibility would be exasperating if the gap is wide. If the guy could predict a tiresome effort, it means that he could face frustrations in future. The agony of change that the bloke could confront might become the source of the imminent problems in the relationship. Therefore, the man may minimise or eliminate complications by adjusting or realising that the painful compromising gap might affect the relationship and mental health of the involved parties. However, the concepts in this book will help men to recognise different ways compatibility can be attained in a relationship. The recommendations in the coming chapters will continue to highlight the importance of compatibility in achieving a satisfying and healthy relationship. The

11

concepts will demonstrate the value of personalities in many romantic situations. Figure 1 is a Personality Identifier Metrics (PIM) that guides men towards understanding their personalities. If men were able to understand their personalities, they would define the mirror image they desire from a woman to achieve compatibility. Additionally, when a guy understands his personality traits, he would also learn his bad habits that might impact on the female lover and subsequently affect the relationship. The simple metrics below highlights an evaluation framework that a man should undertake to understand his personality. The bloke would be able to align the quality of his personality traits to his potential suitor to verify a natural similarity or to enable him to adjust to hers. Since personality traits are rarely 100 per cent similar, a man would be expected to make some adjustments to attain a higher degree of similarity that reflects his potential suitor.

Personality Identifier Metrics

Category	Elements	Level of strength 1-33%	Dominant personality
1	Religious		kind & keeper
	Honesty		
	Patient		
	Total		

Category	Elements	Level of strength 1-33%	Dominant personality
2	Adventrous		Hospitable or Reckless
	Friendly		
	Fun		
	Total		

Category	Elements	Level of strength 1-33%	Dominant personality
3	Political		Assertive or Arrogant
	Academic		
	Opinionated		
	Total		

Category	Elements	Level of strength 1-33%	Dominant personality
4	Rebelious		Inconsiderate
	Moody		
	Impatient		
	Total		

Figure 1: Personality Identifier Metrics

Interpretation

The Personality Identifier Metrics (PIM) figure 1 above helps a man to establish personal characteristics for self-evaluation and to apply when identifying a potential suitor. The above framework comprises of categories that are defined through the degree of strength achieved from personality totals. The individual puts his scores on each element and adds

13

them to obtain totals for each category. The highest totals from each category indicate the dominant personality while the other total scores show the level of influence for each category within the man's total behaviour. A man needs to enter scores with honesty to attain results that reflect his true degree of personality traits. If one category indicates 60% mark or above while others are below 30%, the highest mark shows the individual's dominant trait known as absolute personality. The highest score among the categories indicates the individual's strength of personality from which the analysis would be emphasised. If two or three categories denote relative high scores, the rating would indicate a non-absolute but definable personality traits. If a result produces high scores that include categories 1 and 4, it indicates the scoring may contain untruthful ratings. If relatively high scores were attained among categories 2, 3 and 4, the interpretation indicates negative personalities that define recklessness, arrogance and inconsiderate traits. However, if category 1 is identified alongside 2 and 3, it means positive personality traits that indicate kindness or committed, hospitable and assertiveness. The book provides an Internet link at the end for anyone that needs personal, practical, advanced and automated information about his personality.

Accepting Reality

A man that takes an honest self-introspection can perform a realistic scoring to obtain a reflective outcome. When the dude is committed to undertake a factual process, he would gracefully accept truthful results. A gentleman should understand his objectives before embarking on a self-introspection process. The common objectives for most lads relate to learning and strengthening personality traits that influence behaviour. It should be noted that an analysis might not be performed without accurate results from the self-introspection process. More so, the results may become meaningless if the lad does not accept and acknowledge crucial elements that reveal the true picture of his personality. When a gentleman fails to acknowledge his results, he cannot effectively act on them to gain the desired outcome. If the bloke were determined to achieve desired improvement, he would accept the results and make the necessary adjustments for the sake of falling in love with a compatible person. In most cases, a man that reflects on his personality can work hard to achieve his aspirations. When a person works really hard, he would be able to cherish his effort and the subsequent results. Most women are instinctively capable of evaluating personalities of men. However, some women might identify and knowingly accept men with undesirable personalities to safeguard their own ego. Mostly, some women prefer satisfying their egos through attaining a marriage or an economical security without considering the quality and strength of the relationship. Generally, most loving women desire men that share compatible personality traits. However, the females also encounter challenges to meet prospective suitors that share compatible personality traits.

Females that value safeguards like economical security explain that men with compatible personality traits are rare to find. People that previously faced a challenge to find a compatible lover may not be hesitant to confirm to others that such problems are real. If a person needs to justify reasons for undertaking a personality test, a relevant question would help. A question that might be asked relate to knowing specific characteristic elements that can be improved to project a suitable lover? The honest truth is that most people are incapable of defining their characteristics and that of their potential or current lovers. If people could define their own personality traits from an informed position, they would know why it is difficult for them to find compatible partners. A wise man needs to understand his personality trait to define compatibility so that he does not fall for a person with sinister or incongruous motives. If a man settles for a woman who is merely interested in marriage or economical security regardless of compatible qualities, he is likely to face a challenging marriage. A man that understands personality traits would be able to evaluate a woman's dominant characteristics and verify their matching qualities. Women that take complementary preferences as the only prerequisite disregard the importance of primary needs that focus on compatible traits from the personality perspective. Compatible qualities are traditional or primary issues as they are considered moral values in marriage.

A woman's primary or traditional elements are more important for a man to know so that he could establish if they might be compatible. The starting point for a man to attract the love of the woman is by providing evidence of performing on her secondary desires known as complementary preferences. Complementary preferences are important elements that visibly attract the love of a woman. If a woman's secondary desires are combined with personality traits that are shared with a man, the relationship is likely to be very strong and fulfilling. If a man disregards a woman's ego, his relationship will be as turbulent or unsuccessful as not having compatibility. However, if a man is flattered by the attention given to him only because he can satisfy the woman's secondary desires, he would face problems when his fortunes change for the worst in the future. Mostly, when a lad experiences a change in fortunes, some women would perceive him as impoverished and undesirable. In other words, if the man's dazzling light extinguishes, some women that previously glorified his fortunes would become antagonistic towards him. Thereafter, the man may begin to face a potentially stressful life if a woman only valued something other than his personality traits that he may control.

The list of important elements that cover secondary elements that satisfy a woman's ego is provided in a detailed analysis under the chapter entitled a 'Woman's code". While the list is not exhaustive, it covers major elements that are general and universal. The prominent elements relating to complementary preferences can affect happiness if they are ignored because they are usually the ones that attract women to men. Hence, the complementary preferences are regarded as the code of a woman because they describe her most valuable desires that drive her ego and happiness. Hence, women get attracted to men that competitively show the best performance to satisfy their dreams. Hence, man that are good at performing enable women to achieve the first half of happiness that can be read from the emotional connection. Women achieve the other half of emotional connection form the primary elements of compatibility that brings stability or a sense of belonging in the relationship. Hence, the list below is an introductory summary of the secondary elements from the category C list on the Cluster Dynamic Metrics (CDM).

a. *Vision, Stability and Commitment*

The 'Aspirational Phase' is a stage that allows a man to evaluate his self worth to a serious woman that requires stability and certainty in a romantic relationship. Women would expect to know a man's aspirations from his plans that he would be working on to achieve his goals. In general, every guy has an obligation to provide clarity over his intention to achieve his goals through personal interpretation. Women would begin their evaluation through a man's presentation from the first moment they begin to communicate. However, she would gradually begin to ask questions directly after a month of dating to confirm her assumptions. Women associate aspiration and clear objectives with a stable and visionary mind that can constructively cooperate and build a stable home in a community. Previously, women used to relay on the support of a man that possesses a stable mind. Currently, women's attitudes and opportunities are changing for the better and the idea of relaying on the support from men is gradually being replaced by the need to associate with success.

Hence, women still use their subconscious ability to evaluate and establish the stability of a man's mind through undertaking an effortless assessment of the manner he defines his purpose, demonstrates determination and explains issues with clarity. Sometimes women wilfully test a man's commitment through evaluating his perseverance, respect and tactful pursuit. However, men should understand that women value commitment and stability. Most women expect timely commitment and stability from a man to counteract the impact of age on the biology of bearing children. Most women are only anxious about delaying marriage because of an aging process that gradually diminishes a youthful beauty. A minority of women feel that a diminished youthful beauty impacts on the potential to accomplish an everlasting romantic affection from a serious suitor. Accordingly, women's instinctive desire for commitment and stability evolved to become a relatively common trait that dictates a desire for seriousness from men even where factors of bearing children or marriage are non-existent.

b. Economic status

The economic status is an extension of a visionary cluster and it has been used to highlight relevant issues within a relationship. Traditionally, a man's economic status is considered useful in boosting a woman's interest for a romantic relationship. Increasingly, some women are relegating economic interest from a major position to a less prominent one. Women that relegate economic interest in a relationship still hold their personal financial success in relatively high esteem. The females understand that their own effort towards financial success may be a gift that a compatible partner lacks. As a result, the women my not loss a compatible man and face a miserable life over something they can supplement or cover through their own effort. Hence, females that place economic status at a less prominent position do so to allow other principle variables to boost their romantic interests. Some women are economically successful in their own right or do not value it more than other important factors. People that prefer stability, morals and commitment among other elements may reluctantly consider economic success in conjunction with others that are more relevant. However, when a man is looking for a woman to date and subsequently to marry, it is vital for him to evaluate his current and future economical status. Some women prefer economic stability so that they could live a less stressful life when married or living together. However, economic stability is relative to age and other stages in life. Most men achieve a relatively stable life at ages above 35 or 40 years. Hence, most men will begin to look more self-assured because of economic success that empowers them. However, some men that understand the value of visions and strategies get empowered by knowledge and the prospect of improving lives rather than being driven by financial wealth.

Mostly, people with a vision and strategic plan ooze optimism and contentment. Mostly men suffer a sudden diminished confidence when their financial wealthy is not recognised, appreciated or gets lost. It may not be a problem for such people to rely on the magic of their wealth to again a romantic relationship. However, a person should be able to sustain his wealth if he wants to endlessly continue to enjoy the perks of his success. Some men are lucky to fall in love with women that highly consider wealth in the beginning of the relationship and subsequently begin to value the man more than his riches. If a man loses his riches at a later stage, certain woman would hold dear to other best parts of the relationship.

Other woman may give up a relationship when circumstances behind the loss of his wealth are associated with intolerable factors that impact on their romantic affair. As such, if a man understands his personality, he would devise coping strategies to handle traits of a specific woman he prefers. However, people that expect a young man to be economically stable in his early years of adulthood spell injustice to his persona, intelligence and life journey. Equally, many men that endure the tedious and painful journey over delaying fortunes often face the verdict of nonentity and imprudent. Mostly, men in categorise that include those in struggling business ventures and reskilling for better jobs emotionally get wounded by the disheartening insults over the way they are characterised.

Similarly, lads undergoing divorces are likely to face an economic instability and might face challenges to be seen in 'shimmering light'. It could be illogical for a man to feel victimised and insecure because of people's impressions, perspectives and choices. Since some people's perspectives do not represents a true-to-life situation, it is worth ignoring to focus on future goals.

A man that relies on his mental strength and self-assurance often finds similar woman drawn to him. Once a man presents himself in a confident and intelligible manner, he is likely to attract a woman with similar traits and mannerism. In most cases, a confident and intelligible man is bound to enjoy the experience of being in a relationship with a like-minded person. Men should know that most self-driven women are well informed, supportive, tolerant and patient. If a lad meets a self-driven woman when he is financially strained and without clear, defined and committed future plans, he should not expect sympathy but encouragement. If the woman pushes him to work hard, he should understand the need to excel and make everyone proud. However, men often mistake a passionate and emotional inquiry from women for arrogance and anger. As a result, some men think that women express their feelings in a confrontational, illogical and disrespectful manner. Hence, the misunderstanding between men and women often degenerates into unwarranted antagonism.

If a man realises the woman's passion, he would define his current and future plans in a way that the woman would appreciate. Otherwise the need for sympathy leads some man to become irrational and angry. Most women expect continuous communication to through direct talk and adequate evidence of the effort being applied. Nevertheless, some men that lack knowledge about their future would not know what to communicate.

Males' Complementary Preferences

When a man considers a suitor under the 'Aspirational Phase', his main personality trait becomes his benchmark for the woman he wants to date and possibly marry. However, men also cherry-pick on other elements known as complementary preferences. According to men, complementary preferences improve the perceived degree of compatibility that makes a romantic relationship more enjoyable for them. The complementary choice of facial or body beauty is the main element that overshadows others such as elegance, education, wealth and wittiness. All the complementary preferences often cease to be noticeable when the romantic relationship reaches a maturity stage in its life cycle. The maturity stage of a romantic relationship within its life cycle needs to be continuously sustained to become everlasting. Nonetheless, the complementary choices are usual essential for a man at the initial stages of a romantic affair. Some men realise that complementary elements often disappear with age despite being significantly attractive at the beginning of the relationship.

Few men become obsessed with complementary preferences at the initial stage and ignore the primary elements that lead to a fulfilling romantic relationship. Crucially, some men ignore bad indications at the beginning of a relationship in favour of elements such as beauty among others. Eventually, the men encounter miserable lives after worshipping complementary choices. When a man holds complementary preferences in excessively high esteem, he would struggle when the desires fade and become irrelevant to the dynamics in a relationship. Men should regard complementary choices as coated trophies that fade way with age or overtaken by the dynamics in a relationship. Men are visually attracted to a woman's beauty and mentally drown to affiliation, elegance, education, wealth and wittiness. It should be emphasised that a man should avoid becoming a victim of his obsessions. However, an in-depth description of a major complementary preference for men is explained to acknowledge its value to a successful relationship.

Facial and Body

Arguably, a person's beauty does not have a universally agreed standard, as some people believe that beauty is in the eyes of beholder. Men perceive beauty differently because of socialisation, exposure and personal preferences. Many different communities prefer a specific model of beauty. Hence, women from different communities use specific methods to beautify their faces in a way that conforms to a specific model. Women from villages in Sub-Saharan countries apply make-up on their faces using natural ingredients and some traditional methods to create the visual beauty preferred in their societies. Equally, women from villages across Asia and South America among others also use methods that make them look more beautiful and appealing to their communities. Women from affluent societies are also using modern technology to change their body and facial appearances. The women's effort to alter or add cosmetics to their bodies indicates their need to look beautiful to the society or peers that appreciate them. As a result, men appreciate the beauty they are exposed because they get accustomed to familiar models in that society. Hence, most men are influenced in defining beauty by socialisation. Men can deviate from the society's model of beauty when they get exposed or aspired to believe in a different kind of beauty.

However, men's preference for beauty has many variations despite conforming to a general or master framework. Sometimes a person's perception of beauty my change with time because of influences such as age, weight, size of body features and health among other variables. Men that are open-minded do not restrict their choices to a particular model of beauty. The men that are open-minded about women's beauty arguably experience the best from a wide option to choose a possible suitor. Some men loose opportunities when they get fixated on a specific model of beauty and fail to change their preference. When a woman possesses compatible personality traits without the desired appearance, most men will never adjust. Most men value attraction because of the sexual power that overrides the importance of personality traits to compatibility. Few men that half-heartedly accept a different form of beauty to what they prefer are likely to present a challenging behaviour against women they choose on the basis of compatible personality traits. It has been found that some men tend to disrespect woman they half-heartedly choose.

The men would develop a lack of elements such as devotion, admiration and respect because they woman does not look attractive. A man needs to devote wholeheartedly to a woman if he aspires for happiness, fulfilment and an everlasting relationship after he has made his choice. It is imperative to understand that beauty comes in different forms. If men were capable of looking beyond a specific form of appearance, they would

24

provide themselves with a rare opportunity to explore the hidden and exotic beauty that love offers. It is important to be drawn to a potential suitor that pursues grooming and physically fitness than preferring extreme facial beauty and perfect body structure than are cosmetic than natural. Equally, men have a role to support their lovers by getting involved in grooming and pursuing physically fitness. If men develop a preference for grooming and pursuing physically fitness among other complementary elements, extreme beauty would not be a priority.

Comment

It was revealed that the aspirational phase is essential for providing a man an opportunity to evaluate and improve his optimism towards attaining and nurturing a romantic relation that fulfils his ambition. The chapter indicates that the aspirational phase is vital for men to recognise their capacity and understand the unique challenges that may prevent them from achieving the rare fulfilment in romantic relationships. The most obvious challenges compel men to harnessing opportunities to improve their knowledge and skills that help to attain an everlasting and satisfactory romantic experiences. Thus, a man that possesses a progressive and king mentality is expected to refrain from being deceitful and debasing the dignity of a woman he professes to love. It was highlighted that a man's preferences should mostly be reflective of his persona. Furthermore, the man should be consistent and truthful if he wants a woman to accept some of his shortcomings. If a man is disloyal, the vibe he radiates is likely to deflect back to him through a woman's reaction. Therefore, a man needs to be honest, respectful and secure in order for the aspirational phase to prepare him for a possible future success in a romantic relationship.

If a man identifies the undesirable traits he possesses, it would be best to dive straight into the training process to possibly push for the desired change. It should be reiterated that an aspirational phase helps to change objectionable traits. If a man improves his persona, he would exponentially advance his prospect of becoming a potential suitor to a likeminded woman.

Men should realise that if they disregard their astuteness and relative improvements, they endanger the sweetness of being loved in equal return. Some people convincingly argue that women's complexion of love is different that of men. It is stated that men thrive when immeasurably respected with tenderness while women blossom when treasured and sexually desired. However, men need to realise that the spirit of love is the essence of projected feeling that should be incessantly and abundantly given without hesitation. Thus, a like-minded woman would be attracted to the charms of a man whose confidence is projected through his behavioural traits. Women instinctively fear that a man's insecurity could become a source of complications in the relationship. Hence, men need to become conscious of their position when they encounter unbearable change noticeable in the lack of kindness, unfathomed resistance, rudeness or hostility from the purported suitor.

Chapter 3

Spotting phase

Men should make it mandatory to build and strengthen their own goals at the aspirational stage to succeed in spotting a potential suitor. A man needs to be serious when it comes to achieving positive attributes. His seriousness can be demonstrated through diligently applying the Personality Identifier Metrics. The tool reveals strong evidence-based elements that strengthen personality traits to apply in searching for a fulfilling relationship with an appropriate woman. The Personality Identifier Metrics also saves as a motivating tool for men to acquire relevant knowledge that helps to change, improve and reinforce positive attributes on their personalities. More so, the Personality Identifier Metrics helps a man to deduce more qualities about the female he expects to enjoy a fulfilling and everlasting romantic relationship. When a man could define characteristics of the suitable woman, he can possibly deduce the place she might enjoy visiting. Many studies indicate that people are likely to enjoy visiting places that satisfy the value of their characteristics. Therefore, most modern men should be able to identify places they might potentially find women of particular characteristics. Hence, the descriptions of educational institutions, work and business environments, social places, family and friends settings and social media will explain the importance of specific meeting places known to be of major interest.

Educational institutions

Educational institutions are among the most common places that likeminded people can meet after evaluating complementary preferences and compatibility values. There are various activities within the institutions that provide opportunities for people to meet and engage in a conversation to determine complementary preferences and compatibility values. People might meet during activities such as sports and hobbies among others as an opportunity to socialise and acquaint with people. These places allow conversations that might provide interesting hints for chemistry, compatibility and other preferences that help a relationship to become fulfilling and everlasting. Mostly, educational institutions are among appropriate places a man could identify a woman. The environments fairly rated among the best places a man might meet a sober personality likely to conform to a desired decent stature. Thus, a place that provides a sober and mature atmosphere usually makes people relatively friendly and accessible while exposing their respect for constructive engagement.

Educational environments also provide the ability for an individual to live under conventional rules in specific situations. Equally, educational institutions provide opportunities for people to learn about a person's principles that form the basis for compatibility. Equally, people's independent spirit while staying or attending lessons at an educational institution gives an opportunity to others to establish the individual's level of rigidity or flexibility. There are many people that can happily relate to experiences they encountered in high school, colleges, universities and training centres among others. When students stay or attend lessons at an educational institution, they are normally exposed to diverse groups of people. As such, some individuals can use the opportunity to search for a suitable person. Students have an advantage to learn without the world being judgmental about their freedom while still actively attached to an educational institution. Hence, educational places provide people with opportunities to clearly evaluate a likely suitor that might fulfil a dream for a lasting romantic relationship.

Work and Business Environments

Many people arguably believe in positive outcomes experienced from work or business environments. Work or business environments allow people to meet possible suitors that might ordinarily be ready to fulfil an everlasting romantic quest. In particular, work or business places offer opportunities for people to communicate and explore favourable and sociable characteristics that may lead to a fulfilling romantic connection. It is mostly assumed that work or business colleagues are likely to begin engaging in a conversation with a sense of dynamism, professionalism, intellectual and social competency. The quality of conversations provides opportunities for people to explore relationship possibilities that may develop into a strong connection.

Nevertheless, it is important to be aware of the demerits of searching for a possible suitor at places of work or business. There are laws and ethics that might prevent people from pursuing romantic relations at work. In particular, people are more prone to face sexual harassment laws relating to their behaviour against work colleagues. The laws are important for employees, managers and owners to know and understand them. Sexual harassment law is enacted to prevent advances or connotations of sexual nature that are considered inappropriate. Sexual harassment acts are unwanted advances that make the victim uncomfortable or offended. Generally, sexual harassment is more pronounced when a powerful person, mostly at senior level makes advances or sexual connotations to junior member of staffs.

In such cases, the actions of a perpetrator are perceived as abuse of power against a weak individual. According to the interpretation of the law, it is believed that a perpetrator would have made the advances with the full knowledge that the subordinate may have no choice. The law entails that a weaker individual would be afraid to resist because of possible repercussions. Hence, the weaker person might only accept romantic advances in anticipation of opportunities for promotion, pay increase or other work benefits. Conversely, the victim might feel forced to accept advances or connotations of sexual nature for fear of losing her job. Business environments such as seminars, conferences and other types of meetings present a conundrum to some men that may see a potential suitor at such forums. There is an increasing number of women that want to be regarded in professional terms when taking part in business or professional environments. Some men may assume that if they approach the women with respect, their actions would be tolerated. As a sign of protest, some women feel that their gender worked hard to attain the respect they deserve in business. The women feel that if they allow men to sexualise them during business hours or occasions, they will be actively participating in reversing the gains achieved by feminists. However, some women would not be offended by an approach from men that seem mature, restrained, respectful and skilful.

The women realise that there are opportunities for likeminded people to meet in business places. Therefore, the women are comfortable to offer the opportunities to approaching on matters related to building a romantic relationship. Equally, the women do not see anything wrong to either accept or amicably turn down any flattering advances relating to building a romantic relationship with the men. Some men are luck to have met women that are good at registering displeasure in a gentle manner. Nonetheless, men have an obligation to desist from an immature and disrespectful behaviour towards women. Men that use emotional intelligence are good at exercising patience, tolerance and composure when approaching women. As such, the business environment validates the importance of being attuned to the 'Personality Identifier Metrics' and the 'Cluster Dynamic Metrics' that improve men's understanding of women. Men's personal weaknesses are likely to be drastically improved if the individual is committed, truthful, humble and keen to learn. Equally, when men identify their strengths, the tools give them an opportunity to reinforce and maintain advantages from their personalities. A man that accurately and efficiently applies the tools is bound to strengthen his communication skills and effectively improve his emotional intelligence. The tools will help the man to learn to adjust his behaviour according to social, professional and business settings. Nevertheless, it should be restated that business and professional environments are increasingly becoming challenging for people that may want to start a romantic and respectful affairs because of moral, ethical and legal concerns.

Social Places

Men would face less stringent benchmarks in social places compared to business related environments that require serious adherence and attention to laws, morals and ethics. Every man knows that societies require orderly conduct that promotes harmony, respect and relative freedoms. If societies do not effectively promote orderly conduct, principles and structures will crumble and behavioural challenges will take control. Hence, people are obliged to identify specific practices allowed in each place they visit. Therefore, men need to understand that places such as churches, parks, night and social clubs among others are associated with different moral, ethical and legal principles. Nevertheless, all social settings allow people to share relaxed, friendly and enjoyable atmospheres. Social settings naturally make people feel happier, relaxed and flexible. Some people visit social places to refresh, entertain and improve their moods from challenging personal circumstances.

Men should be aware of impolite people they may encounter in social places. When some individual are facing challenges in their personal life, they can be rude. Few individuals among the unhappy ones can only be discourteous if unintelligently befriended. However, most social spaces are considered best rendezvous for people that want friendly associations with likeminded individuals. Therefore, it is important for a man to apply his best personality traits that he identified and improved after tabulating his scores on the Personality Identifier Metrics. A confident man is more restrained and tolerant when he faces a woman that expresses her displeasure in an unflattering or debasing manner. When a man is faced with an unappealing experience, he should not demean the value of social places or overreact as it also damages his dignity. People shall continue to treasure social places for their advantages pertaining to social experiences.

Family & Friendship Settings

A man that holds clarity over the type of woman he wishes to meet and fall in love is capable of describing her to his family and friends. Friends and family have a wider reach of people and may provide recommendations within their large networks. A person may not be aware of some of his best characteristics know by his family and friends. Equally, an individual may benefit from the honest assessment from his family and friends that he knew but never wanted to admit. Hence, many people abhor depictions of their characteristics from friends and family because of their brutal honesty. Some men may subconscious avoid assessments that might be infuriating or ugly. Most people do not realise that being in denial affect would severely deprive them of an everlasting happiness. It is worth considering the opinions of family and peers to extract the best that they can offer.

However, it is also possible that family and friends may mischaracterise or disregard the best values of a man in favour of their misperceptions, ignorance or vindictiveness they covertly present for consideration. Therefore, a man retains the right to cautiously accept or sensibly decline any help offered to him. A man should feel resolutely motivated to achieve happiness and fulfilment. His determination can be demonstrated through comparing opinions from family and friends with the outcome of the analysis he undertook using the Personality Identifier Metrics. If a man applies impartiality in process he employs to achieve the best results, he will realise the importance of his invested effort when unimaginable outcomes are endlessly enjoyed. Sometime a man has to give a reasonable degree of trust to family and friends in order for him to enjoy the growth and journey of life.

The Internet

The Intent is used to access social networks and dating sites that provide a wide pool of opportunities for people to meet across the globe. Social networks and other dating sites have been growing so rapidly because of the massive benefits they provide to honest and determined people. The Internet provides opportunities for people that might not have met due to differences in geographic locations. People that live very far apart do not usually meet by chance. If the individuals had met, they may never have spoken to each other as strangers. Similarly, people that live close to each other rarely meet and if they do, they remain strangers unless unforeseen circumstances bring them to talk. In the few occasions that strangers with compatible interests meet, a handful would be brave to begin a conversation. Even those that would communicate may become hesitant to push it further towards the potential to date. Some men do not have the ability to approach and befriend another individual. More so, the same men may not dare express their interest to women after being befriended for a relatively long period. Mostly, the lads lack general charisma despite the women giving them opportunities to express their feelings. When some men coincidently meet desirable women, they are often too formal, nervous and far removed from showing any interest towards laying a foundation for a potential relationship.

Chapter 4

Internet Characteristics

Internet platforms use relatively new technology to help people that seek to win dates in convenient ways. It is important to understand how the platforms are helpful to most people seeking dates from potential lovers. The platforms changed the way people make their initial contact. The characteristics of the platforms make them more relevant to a modern way of establishing initial contact. The Internet platforms can be intimidating, confusing and dangerous if an individual does not understand their characteristics. If people around the world were all sincere, considerate and steadfast, individuals would focus on one characteristic relating to convenience. However, the characteristics of Internet platforms continue to increase because more dubious means continue to be discovered from some users with evil intent.

If all people were genuine, the convenience of initial contact would have remained the main focus for people that seek dates from potential lovers. Naively, people still consider the convenience of making the initial contact the most important element than the other factors that continue to emerge from the use of platforms. There are so many characteristics to consider when registering and making or replying to an initial contact. People have to consider accepting the first and subsequent dates after undertaking adequate analysis using the platforms' characteristics. Therefore, individuals have a duty to understand the characteristics of the platforms in order to protect their interest, dignity and health. Many people blindly engage the Internet platforms and the potential suitors before considering the potential impact to their wellbeing.

People would reduce risks if they apply measures to protect their safety. While the platforms were created for people to communicate with the wider public, they carry some risks to some innocent individuals that use them. It is important for individuals to realise that dating is an emotional matters. As a result, malicious people take opportunities to harass or cause emotional damage that impact on one's health. People that are ignorant or evil prey on individuals' fragility to love. People take advantage of the platforms' inevitable use of attractive language to lure potential lovers. Success cannot be achieved on the platforms if the profile does not convince other individuals that they are the best potential suitor.

A person can enjoy the first success if the potential suitor allows them to engage in a communication process. The second part of the success can be achieved when given an opportunity to go for a first date. The third achievement is gained when subsequent dates are achieved with the same person. The fourth and final achievement is marked when the individuals become lovers. As such, there are dangers associated with every stage of the process. Therefore, when using the Internet platforms for dating, individuals need to apply due diligence to protect the emotional impact to their health and wellbeing. Unless individuals examine the characteristics of the Internet platforms using a Due Diligence System on figure 2, people will continue to face emotional and physical risks. This chapter focuses on dissecting characteristics of dating sites and social networks to improve safety and dating success.

Dating sites

Dating sites resolve may problems for most men and women that are inconvenienced by different things. Individuals that are always busy may not afford time to visit and socialise in places with many people. Equally, persons that live in isolated places do not often get opportunities to interact with different individuals. Similarly, many people believe in casting their nets wider to seek the best partners. Importantly, dating sites bring a different dimension to few individuals that are usually hesitant to initiate meaningful conversations with strangers. As such, dating sites provides chances for people with congruous interest to meet in carefully chosen platforms. People that make contact through dating sites have their intentions predefined by the nature of the platform that brings them together to communicate and subsequently date. The power of dating sites is in the presentation containing carefully articulated information. The profile presentation for each individual is intended to draw the attention of a potential suitor. When people register on dating sites, they attempt to persuasively express their interests in order to attract the responsiveness of equally fascinating persons.

Dating sites provide a relatively protected platform that increases a chance for likely suitors to meet and possibly fall in love. The Personality Identifier Metrics (PIM) and the Cluster Dynamics (CDM) are effectively useful in helping people to clearly define and post relevant information on their profiles. If a man is armed with honest, appropriate and convincing information, he can achieve his goals on a reputable site. However, dating sites do not provide snooping opportunities for potential suitors that need more information before contacting the individual. People that register on dating sites post limited information because of a restrictive structure. As such, men that use dating sites without the aid of the PIM and the CDM tools face challenges in trying to creatively provide information that could be effectively impressive. The information structures on dating sites do not completely offer measures that prevent dishonest people from posting deceitful information. As a result, the few people that are dishonest are able to waste other individuals' precious time. Deceitful people are capable of posting information that projects a false image on their profiles. Mostly, dishonest people are not concerned about destroying the reputation of dating sites. People that are deceitful do not have a reputation to protect and are obsessed with destroying the image of others. Few ignorant people do not realise that billions of people are benefiting from the convenience offered by dating sites. Facebook is among many social networks that offer a better chance for snooping to gather information about a potential suitor. Dating sites present a challenge in that they offer restricted and carefully edited information than social networks. There are instances where people can suspect an effort from a profile owner that attempted to clean up profile information in order to present a better impression on social networks like Facebook.

Social Networks

Mostly, people post many photos and comments over a long period of time on social networks such as Facebook. As such, Facebook profiles offer an opportunity to be doubtful when the person exhibits an inconsistent or undesirable pattern of behaviour. Ordinarily, the authenticity of a person can be judged from the company of his or her close associates. Before people arrange to meet, it might be safer to first understand a bit of the other person's personality from the social media profile. Nevertheless, some people are good at sustaining a deceiving narrative over a long period. People that are seasoned deceivers can perpetuate a carefully orchestrated narrative using inaccurate but fanciful impression about their persona for a period of 2 years. People need to be careful about the projected image when using social media for dating purposes. Every individual should consider the idea of undertaking a thorough investigation to try and understand the nature of an individual they intend to date. Each individual needs to realise that investigations of such kind are not concluded from a quick perusal. People have to learn that the best investigation outcome can be concluded from many as three perusals and analysis to become relatively satisfied. When investigating, people can achieve milestones by mentally organising data derived from the profile. The outcome from analysing organised data helps to establish a pattern of behaviour.

Mostly, the three milestones to be achieved relate to information that can be gathered to provide a general idea about the individual being investigated. It is important to repeatedly peruse so that scrutiny can be thorough. If the scrutiny is meticulous, the person snooping can establish the pattern of behaviour. The best behaviour from a profile should illustrate consistence, acceptability and above reproach. The first type of scrutiny is called a photo story, which relates to pictures posted on a profile page of a social network. The profile page should feature a multitude of photos in different places with friends and relatives. If a profile page has few photos, the authenticity of the page or the person becomes questionable. Equally, if the few photos are duplicated and repeatedly presented, it may means that the owner intended to falsify the profile to interested stakeholders. Similarly, if the posted photos do not feature any friends and family, it may be assumed that the profile page was created with a sinister motive. When a person features a page with photos that do not bear any resemblance, it indicates a fake or dubious character behind the profile. The second quest for scrutiny relates to what is known as an active indicator. If a person undertakes the initial contact through social media, it means that the profile should currently be very active.

Due Dilegence Systems

▲ Photo Story
△ Profile Age
▲ Activity

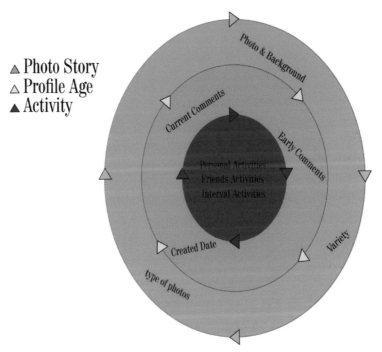

Figure 2: Due Diligence System

Typically, most suspicious profiles are newly created and lack a relatively frequent participation from friends and families. Therefore, a profile can be active if it shows posts covering more than two years to current period. People can identify if the profile owner is active on her page through dates shown on posts and relevant comments. Equally, if the profile owner posts photos showing different places over a longer period, it indicates that the profile page has been active for a number of years. More so, a profile page that shows photos with different backgrounds that denote places, it shows that the person is active on the social network and in real life. As such, a profile page needs to be active to give a relatively detailed story of an individual from which personality traits can be unpicked. The thirty type of scrutiny is called information volume because of its focus on quantity. A profile needs to contain more information for others to deduce the characteristic nature of the person.

A profile that also features limited photos of one individual with very few comments or reactions from close acquaintances and family means that the profile owner may not be trustworthy. Likewise, the amount and quality of her responses to friends' comments indicate if the person is reliable. Also, people with abnormal number of friends for none celebrity or too few friends below a normal person of the same age need their profiles validated through a serious personality analysis. At the same time, if a profile owner has an abnormal number of friends from the opposite sex, it entails that the profile may not be real or the examiner needs to carry out an in-depth personality analysis. When a man undertakes snooping, he needs to realise that the aim is only to build an initial character impression from the profile. Men should exercise control by refraining from developing bad habits such as becoming obsessed with snooping or stalking on the social network. However, dating sites and social media are currently the best channels of contact. Internet sources are more helpful in initiating contact and verifying personality traits of individuals. When a man undertakes controlled snooping and communicating under initial investigations, he is likely to deduce personality traits and authenticity.

Chapter 5

Approaching Phase

Many men struggle to understand the thoughtful process of some women during the first stages of making contact. Men face the first challenges because they fail to recognise that the initial form of contact determines the quality of response from women. Therefore, it is imperative to provide the analysis according to different contexts that underpin the initial form of contact. According to men that were interviewed, they stated that some responses could depend on age, culture, religion, place, frequency and economical contexts among others. Naturally, when people make the initial contact, they are less likely to have information about each other. Hence, some people create unsubstantiated assumptions about another person because of appearance or how they met.

Response types

Initial responses are important to anyone that seeks a person they feel they could possibly develop a strong connection. Traditionally, initial responses are encountered only when people meet and communicate face to face for the first time. The advent of technology enables some people to communicate before they meet. People have a role to create interest before communicating and subsequently arrange a date. It is now common knowledge that men measure their incremental success in gradual milestones. Men know that a positive initial response is more important because it determines the potential for achieving the next step towards more opportunities for communication and subsequent dating. However, a man needs to understand the use of a suitable communication strategy that gives a positive initial response. The way people meet determines an appropriate strategy to employed so as to achieve the desired success. Therefore, men need to understand methods of initial contact and the strategies associated with them in order to attain the best initial responds. Increasingly, more people are using the Internet for initial contact although social places still play a significant role in face-to-face meeting. Nevertheless, some people still value the traditional method because of the magnetic and enigmatic experience of the first encounter when none of the persons have prior knowledge of the other. Nonetheless, it is important to begin by understanding the value of the initial response if the first contact is made through any Internet platforms.

Internet response

When people establish contact on a dating site, it is obvious that they are both looking forward to starting a romantic relationship. The initial form of contact on a dating site would be fairly straightforward and unambiguous to both parties. Dating sites allow both parties to immediately begin exploring prospects of developing a romantic relation. People provide profile information they presume would be informative and appealing on a dating site. The 'internet rendezvous' also enables both parties to start verifying points they have already read or been told.

Dating sites response

In most cases, dating sites increase chances of parties being polite and friendly during the initial contact stage. Normally, people become discouraged from responses that fail to make positive impression. Dating sites make people fearless to withdraw from trying to develop a romantic relationship that may never be fulfilling. However, the quality of a dating site might also determine the quality of response in the initial stage of contact. Dating sites that attract professionals or people of similar stature are mostly known for meticulously vetting members. The sites are continuously assessed, improved and managed to remain effective, friendly and safe. As such, Dating Sites that do not have rigorous vetting system and without robust policies are likely to register people that are rude, inconsiderate and disrespectful. Mostly, the response of individuals provides an indication of the type of their persona.

If a man receives impolite responses in the initial stages, he should not be naïve to think that future experience with the person is likely to be peaceful. It should be noted that some people are excellent at pretending to be good and friend. Hence, if the first respond is flattering, it is important for the individual to analysis consistence in the succeeding communication opportunities. Women are flattered polite, respectful and charming initial contacts or responses. If the person's initial contact or response appears flat and boring, he usually looses an opportunity for further communication and possible date. Mostly, if the dating site was chosen using the knowledge acquired from the Personal Identifier Metrics, a potential suitor is likely to get the gist of the man's communication style if he applies his best.

Social network response

The quality of initial response might be different for those that establish contact through social network. People on social networks might respond after checking the profile of the person they wish to engage. Some women might response harshly or offensively if the social network is mainly a platform for people looking for friendship than to establish a romantic relationship. In some cases, other women might respond in a polite, flattering and friendly way when contacted on social network. The women that may respond in a considerate manner may feel honoured to receive a gesture of appreciation despite lacking an interest in the man. However, men should not be disappointed when a response appears discourteous. Some women distrust men in general because allegedly, they usually take a courteous response for an encouragement to push his luck further.

Some women argue that when a polite response appears on paper, it gives a wrong impression compared to a reply given in a face-to-face contact. Hence, people further argue that the traditional initial contact where individuals meet and talk in person could be more effective than messaging. The proponents of the traditional prefer the potential to observe a facial and verbal reaction than waiting to go on a date with an unworthy person. Some people find messaging to be easier if one is able to deduce a personality from an individual's profile. Those that prefer messaging state that time can be saved from going for a date if personality can be established quickly from the profile. Social networks provide an opportunity to derive a bit of a person's personality trait from the quality, sense and mood of the language. Furthermore, the nature of a person's

46

response or contact can easily be linked to the profile page story to deduce the persona of the individual.

Most times when a person does not receive a response, it usually means that the individual's attention was drawn to personal challenges or other more demanding issues. Nonetheless, it is important for a man to polish his profile, language and other variables in order to project the best from his personality. Most good people perform poorly because of their inability to present the best from their personality. People that articulate their personality effectively are able to sell the best from their traits without lying or exaggerating any of their strong elements. The words that people use can potential carry some prejudicial undertones that may offend the potential suitor. Therefore, men need to be accustomed to the language that draws the attention of women. Equally, people that take too long to respond to a message reduce their chances to develop a romantic relation with a possibly suitable partner.

Similarly, individuals unknowingly destroy novelty appeal created in the initial contact or response phase. People are usually fascinated by the awesomeness newness associated with the initial contact or response phase. As a result, some people love to endlessly enjoy without realising that they would be creating a player image. Consequently, a woman will gain the impression that the man's lack of seriousness shows the reluctance to develop a meaningful relationship. When men prolong the initial contact phase, they destroy the desire for the woman to develop a romantic relationship with enthusiasm.

Place of frequent Visit

People often become familiar with individuals around places they often visit. Mostly when people become familiar with each other, they gradually tend to choose to engage in friendly chats. Commonly, people are predisposed to friendly responses when they become familiar to each other in their usual environments. It is easy for individuals to feel as if they became acquaintances when they are used to seeing each other. It seems natural that most people subconsciously begin to gravitate towards each other the more they see on another. The behaviour of patrons is usual evidenced at workplaces, gyms, small suburban shops, worshiping places and educational institutions among others. Per se, common environments offer chances for individuals to receive positive or polite responds.

A person that respectfully begins to speak to others often receives a welcoming response. Apart from familiarity on its own bringing so many benefits, a person that combines it with maturity finds people responding to him in an openhearted manner. In some cultures, people exchange greetings when they pass each other or congregate at same place. The cultures held by some societies also enable people to go beyond exchanging greeting. When people in those societies become more familiar from seeing and exchanging greetings, they begin to find it easier to extend to conversations. As such, it can be agued that a person's level of maturity and cultural influence has a bearing on the quality of response despite a woman's lack of interest in starting a relationship. A man's chances of receiving positive responds are strengthened if he speaks

48

courageously, confidently, eloquently, intelligently and skilfully. A charming and polite man is more likely to derive respect form women he approaches. More so, a charming, convincing and brave man is usually able to handle rejection with dignity. Men should also note that most women do not like to give the impression that they are easily accessible to anyone. Hence, a man is supposed to apply his communication skill, often considered to be an important asset for achieving considerable success with women. It is every man's desire to gain a warm and encouraging reaction.

Communicating Skills

Human beings understand that communication skills form the backbone of success in every relationship. Surprisingly, communication remains ineffective amongst most people and the challenges are causing the failure of most relationships. Therefore, a man should learn, improve and demonstrate his communication skill to make headways in achieving his set of goals. The men's goals should all be directed at establishing and holding a firm relationship. When men fail to exercise considerable eloquence from the initial stage of contact, he would likely create a negative impact to the foundation of the relationship. People normally underestimate the power of fluency normally demonstrated through creative communication and delivered by verbal, body expression or gestures among other methods. Notably, a man's eloquence can be identified from exercising formal or informal communication. If a woman fails to understand the message, it means the man would be an incompetent communicator.

When a woman decides that there is mutual understanding, it means that the man happens to be an excellent communicator. Furthermore, a man that articulates his interest in an romantic, smooth, passionate and hearts grabbing manner gets to win a million times over with the woman. If a man fails to introduce a conversation in a way that draws attention, he would come across as boring, unintelligent and unwitty. However, some people are gifted at attracting attention through the use of light jokes. Light and intelligent jokes normally commands attention and invoke laughter. Most people that use jokes to 'break the ice' understand the ingenious power of making others laugh. Jokes are among the oldest tricks that skilful men tactfully use to start a conversation. There are few people that can use jokes to 'break the ice', as the majority should avoid causing an embarrassment to their dignity. It should be reiterated that the norms in one society are different from the other. In some societies, it is considered abnormal for a person to begin a conversation with a stranger in any public place.

Communities that experience abductions and other criminal ways discourage women from responding to any unknown male for fear of endangering their safety. Generally, specific social places make people feel friendlier and can easily engage in conversations. However, men should know that some women have moments they dislike any disruption to their peace. People detest disruption if they are tired, stressed or moody and can only engage when their temperaments subside. Therefore, it is not always a man's inability to communicate that makes a woman inaccessible. It does not matter if a man's approach sounds intelligent, jovial and dignified. As long as she is in a different frame of mind, she will remain inaccessible until her circumstances change. However, sometimes some men may exude irresistible aura and her seemingly inaccessible attention can undoubtedly be drawn.

Techniques

It has been made clear that a man's tactical approach usually determines the quality of initial response from a woman. Furthermore, it was pointed out earlier that the quality of initial response also depends on the means of contact and the place for initial meeting. Conversely, when people already know each other as friends, acquaintances or merely familiar through visiting similar places at the same time, they still need a tactical approach to engage or introduce a serious conversation. When people have been friends for a long time, a bid to begin a romantic relationship could be dismissed as a mere joke. Some women would assume that a male friend maybe testing her looseness or stupidity by requesting to enter into a romantic relationship. Therefore, a man has to employ a tactful approach by being direct. A man could also try to create a hypothetical question that would not involve the two friends to test the morality and normality of his hidden feelings towards her. If poorly phrased, the approach may sound unwise, dull and harmful to the friendship.

The effort might be directed at drawing an example of a friendship that turned into a romantic relationship. A teaser story often helps gauge interest before directly introducing the subject. A good approach does not disrupt the existing friendship after failing the attempt to enter into a romantic relationship. Many people are capable of constructing ingenious ways to introduce and assess interest on the subject. However, a person needs to demonstrate seriousness towards a firm position. Equally, some

51

women might not respond immediately due to disbelief. Other people would want an opportunity to deliberate on the issue before indicating their position. Hence, they would expect the man to repeat the issue on a different day or occasions so that they gradually process it. In some instances, a lady might not expect a specific man to consider a romantic relationship with her. It would obviously surprise or confuse her and she might not know how to immediately respond. Some men would wrongly assume that the woman is not keen on starting a romantic relationship.

Yes, if a woman gives an unfriendly response, it usually means that she is not amenable to the idea with the man at that given time. In a case where a female delays showing any interest, a man might identify some cues from her. The man has a choice to demonstrate his willpower for starting a respectable romantic relationship with her. However, if a man receives a friendly response and possible a phone number, it indicates a positive sign. Some women display subconscious hesitation in their behaviour and it takes a courageous, skilful or accustomed man to demonstrate genuineness through a reasonable pursuit.

Men need the awareness and conscience to understand woman's cues and verbal responses that sometimes baffle her too. Mostly, some women face indecision due to self-proclaimed pressure to find elements of major interests on the men. A man has to provide a strong hint as to why the woman should fall for him. If a man fails to minimise the woman's difficulty in making a decision, she may choose the easiest option. Normally, most women find rejecting men's advances to be the easiest option given the experience they might have over many years. Most men are not accustomed to women's cues and they are likely to misread indecisiveness for either total rejection or complete acceptance.

When rejection is quickly assumed, the man is likely to give up. A premature exit may mean that the man felt to have lost a potential suitor. However, some men may continue to rigorously pursue an evidently disinterested woman. When a man undertakes a supposedly reasonable pursuit, he needs to realise and avoid stalking. Stalking is a bothersome conduct or a form of harassment legislated as a criminal behaviour in many parts of the world. Every man or individual should be attuned to facts relating to stalking to prevent violating the rights of others. Some men that are obsessively indifferent to women's needs are likely to engage in stalking. However, if a female responses by accepting the man's request, it allows him to take her on a date. A man honoured with a date would feel that his chance to mesmerize her with his charms has been boosted. A woman also expects a man she gave an opportunity for a date to charm her with attire, paying incurred expenses and generally showing his gentleman qualities.

Most women feel honoured when treated in a dignified manner but many men are not accustomed to the practice. A date also helps a man to continue evaluating if the woman falls within the spectrum of his scores the Personal Identifier Metrics (PIM). A guy would need to attract a woman's heart to get a second date and more opportunities to develop a romantic relationship. However, a lad may fail to win the female over if he doesn't understand his personality preferences. Equally, the man may perform poorly on a date if he does not effectively exercise his emotional intelligence. When a man understands his personality preferences and effectively uses his emotional intelligence, his appropriate tactics is likely to win the lady over. The compatibility criteria for men are generally the same from required by their potential suitors. The differences are identified in the degree of intensity over particular elements. A man has a duty to identify the woman's predominant preferences so that he may correctly interpret and exhibit his own traits.

The man can achieve the required performance if his personal scoring on the Personal Identifier Metrics had been realistic. If his assessment skill grows to be good, he is likely to win over a suitable woman to provide everlasting love and happiness. When a man succeeds in getting second and third dates, he can anticipate the next developmental stages to become more fascinating. As such, the next chapter further highlights how men decode the single loving woman so that everlasting and fulfilling relationships can flourish.

Chapter 6

Dating Phase

A woman reads a man's demeanour so well and unless he is conscious of it, it may cost him subsequent dates. Females develop interest from observing a guy that exhibits a natural flare of alertness and sophistication in his presentation to impress them. At the same time, ladies are good at identifying when a man deliberately amplifies his personality traits and complementary elements. If his hyperboles were found out, it would debase his well-intended effort to make a genuine impression. Many females express their desire for a confident and attentive man. Yet some guys unintentionally show arrogance instead of confidence without knowing the difference in the two characteristics. Women can detect a man's arrogance when his ego would be running wild. A guy should control his arrogance by constantly monitoring an overinflated ego. If self-importance or pride can be controlled, a woman could see confidence than arrogance. When a man exercises confidence, certainty and resolute without necessarily feeling like a super human, a woman would see a steady man. Sometimes insecure men overinflate their egos by talking highly about themselves to feel greater or to feel the same as other people. Many females profess that they resent extreme egos that are detectable from men that hype their stature, abilities and possession.

In terms of possession, an egotistic guy believes more in his own or family's wealthy than being humane and unassuming. A block that bases the extreme ego on his abilities believes greatly about what he does best and never stops talking about it. Equally, a man that holds excessive love for his stature cannot believe in anything more than is own attractiveness.

Mostly, men that derive vanity from their stature are committed to their appearances. Therefore, women feel that men with extreme ego value others a lot less and are mostly very selfish. The females believe that their involvement with egotistic men means that they only serve the purpose of appeasing them for as long as the relationship lasts. As such, the women doubt that the relationship can ever last long. The females also know that they would easily be dispensed with for selfish reasons. Women are mostly convinced that extremely egotistic men often end relationships for none substantive matters. More so, the men would never be bothered that they owe an explanation to the other sensible person so as to achieve closure. Therefore, men should deliberately avoid creating false or inflated impressions to boost their ego. Men with egotistic behaviour should know that they actions cause women to become distant for fear of being hurt by lairs and obnoxious men.

Most women that feel dignified, self-accomplished, focused and well informed usually frown at lairs because of their objectionable personalities. If a man displays an unpleasant behaviour, loving and polite women feel mostly intimidated. Mainly, decent women never feel comfortable around an obnoxious person. Men should also understand that some ladies are insecure because they do not approve of their own attractiveness. Mostly, the women are led to doubt their own beauty by the attitude they receive from men and the society at large. When a woman is treated badly, she feels degraded and her spirit would become deflated. If woman notices a disapproval attitude from a man, she may become discouraged from continuing a relation with him. However, most women that encounter debasing experiences will never stop questioning if any man will ever be romantically drawn to her with endless and genuine love. As a result, some women are fixated at improving their appearances in order to look exceptionally beautiful. People generally feel that if they look beautiful, they would become more visible and admirable. However, any intelligent woman also realises that beauty without the right attitude would not drive a man to feel connected or romantically committed to her.

Many ladies are usually in denial and they disbelieve the fact that a bloke could only be attracted to her beauty than the complete person. Women are mostly capable of deducing that the attraction could only be physical rather than emotional. However, few strikingly beautiful women get carried away with attention and ignore the realisation that the male may only want sexual favours. The women would equate sexual attention with love or emotional connection to justify the reasons for continuing with a relationship that would obviously last for a short period. Most often, men begin a relation with a very beautiful woman with the intention to love her. However, the man is usually discouraged by the attitude of the woman that only values her dazzling beauty. A woman with a despicable attitude looses genuine love despite being approached by overzealous but loving men. Once a man identifies a lady's potentially devastating attitude, it is usually rare for his nature to commit his love to her.

The majority of the men end up getting the gratification of a psychological trophy after a sexual encounter with a very beauty woman. In most cases, men that are not passionately and emotionally connected to a female would prefer a fling than anything serious. The man would quickly escape the stressful attitude of the woman after realising her impact on his mental health. The man gets the consolation for achieving a psychological gratification from the sexual encounter. However, men need to realise that despite the woman's bravado, which is supported by the confidence from her beauty, she would be hurt when the relationship ends. Therefore, there is value for men in being able to distinguish a woman's vanity from vulnerability. Equally, it is important for a man to know the basis for a woman's over confidence to understand the best way to love her. The dynamic cluster framework on figure 3 below helps men to understand the basis for some woman's behaviour. If men could understand the value of the clusters, they are likely to be successful in holding a fulfilling and everlasting relationship with a women they lover.

Cluster Dynamic Metrics

Merit Clusters

The Financial cluster		DESIRABLE SCORING
A	*Elements*	1 to 5
	Affordability	
	Sustainability	
	Competitiveness	
	Usability	
	Humbleness	
	TOTAL	

Visionary Cluster		DESIRABLE SCORING
B	*Elements*	1 to 5
	Planner	
	Strategic	
	Leading	
	Organised	
	Ambitious	
	TOTAL	

Confidence cluster		DESIRABLE SCORING
	Elements	1 to 5
	Excitable	
	Eloquent	
	Trustworthy	
	Self-aware	
	Tidy	
C	TOTAL	

After a man finishes to analyse his performance on each of the merit clusters, he will need to go onto the emotional clusters to perform the same process. When the man scores and calculates to find his best performing cluster among the merit group, he will implement the same process for the emotional group. When he completes the calculations and made comparisons on the components in each group to find his best performance for each respective cluster, he will need to compare the overall 5 categories to identify the order of his best performance amongst all. The man would then use the result of the analysis to identify the dominant code of the woman. If his performance on the clusters matches the specific woman holds, it means that he will manage to meet the complementary preferences of the woman. When the lad fails to match any of his best performances with the cluster that attracts and satisfies the desires of the specific woman, it means that he has some adjustments to make to perform. If the man finds that the adjustment to match the woman's code would be impossible, he will need to make alternative choice so that he could achieve a fulfilling relationship with a likeminded woman. Nevertheless, below is a continuation of figure 2 emotional clusters that will ultimately be compared with all the categories to know the best performance of the man on the complementary preferences of a woman that charms her to fall in love.

Emotional clusters

Emotional Intelligence Cluster		DESIRABLE SCORING
	Elements	1 to 5
D	Polite	
	Attentive	
	Humorous	
	Forgiving	
	Accountable	
	TOTAL	

Caring Cluster	DESIRABLE SCORING
Elements	1 to 5
Romantic	
Generous	
Reliable	
Comforting	
Respecting	
TOTAL	

Figure 3: Cluster Dynamics Metrics

Interpretation

The Cluster Dynamic Metrics *figure 4* above is a personal appraisal framework used to evaluate a man's possible performance to attract and fulfil the love of a specific woman through his abilities. As such, men and women can use the tool to appraise their performance by scoring elements in each cluster. It is normally hard for a bloke to understand women's basic desires and attitudes without being told. The ability to charm a lady can be possible if the lad understands her dominant desires from the clusters. If a man knows the desires of women with relative confidence, he would boldly and creatively apply suitable means to charm her. Hence, figure 3 Cluster Dynamic Metrics illustrates the general requirements that a man can use to charm the right woman. Women expect to be charmed in specific ways that are distinctly listed as 4 clusters namely Emotional Intelligence, Caring, Visionary and Confidence, as depicted above.

A Cluster Dynamic Metrics involves 4 categories that represent complementary preferences that women instinctively expect to be satisfied by men when they charm them. Men can evaluate the effectiveness of their charming power through scoring each element to determine the degree of their value. When each element is scored, they are then added up to get total values for every cluster. The highest of the totals could indicate the dominant cluster that may overwhelmingly win a likeminded woman. Therefore, a man that identifies his most dominant cluster gets to know his most charming tool. When he meets a woman, it is important to first establish if his best tool could charm her. If she can remotely be charmed by any of his strong clusters, it means that the relationship might be challenging if at all it ever begins. The clusters offer a man an opportunity to evaluate his chances with a specific woman. When a man evaluates his scores from each respective cluster, it would help him to make a decision after deducing the complementary preference of the woman. His alternative solutions would be based on a decision to adjust or improve his characteristics. When he discovers that their positions are incongruous, his best solution might rest on desisting from pursuing the woman he intended to love unless he could make some improvements.

A decision from a guy can be made after comparing and contrasting his dominant clusters against the complementary preferences that might attract the woman. However, men mostly misconstrue women's complementary preferences for something they believe to be mythical and therefore complicated beyond comprehension. Men in general share the same fallacy about women's behaviour across the world. However, men are further confused when a woman fails to articulate the most treasured interests she values from a man who would get the greatest chance to win her love. As a result, most lovers coexist in a periodic whirlwind of confusion that often degenerates into serious conflicts. Hence, each of the 4 clusters that comprise of 5 elements provides the desired clarity to eradicate the confusion or misunderstandings. The figure 3 is a framework that helps people to identify and understand the classified elements attributed to respective category that give absolute value or meaning to complementary elements cherished by most women. If men could understand the elements in each basic cluster, they would adjust their levers and successfully promote endless and harmonious love. Men cannot solidly hold a relationship if they neglect women's complementary values like emotional intelligence, caring, visionary and confidence.

Women always feel that men inaccurately define their complementary values in simplistic terms. As a result, women feel that men treat their desire for complementary values with contempt as if the demands are irrelevant and stupid. As such, males are ignorant of their faults when accused of failing to make their women endlessly happy. Of course, there are some women that cannot accurately identify the source of their strength and motivation when in love. Similarly, a handful of females are less satisfied when they realise that their major cluster would be enormously hard for specific man to fulfil it. Therefore, guys that are knowledgeable about identifying clusters have a duty to explain to a woman so that the matter is openly discussed. When the lad attempts or gets the opportunity to discuss the issue, he expects the matter to be clarified so as to resolve differences. If her preferences were insurmountable, the man would decide on the best course of action to take in order for him to enjoy life without regrets. However, if people could realise the importance of every element that shapes each cluster, they would work hard to satisfy them. It would also mean that the women's complementary values that are considered as insurmountable could be adjusted to achieve a compromise where it is possible. The relevant elements can be negotiated to achieve a strong compromise. Women guard their complementary values more jealously than men. Most men are less engrossed with their complementary preferences because of elements that can easily be adjusted or discarded in favour of something more applicable for a new conviction. Hence, the book offers a tool that helps men to understand, score, evaluate, improve and consider elements in each cluster that meet woman's needs.

A man needs to commence the process of employing the tool to help him take essential steps towards charming and fulfilling the needs of a woman in a relationship. Therefore, a man that knows the quality of each element in his behavioural trait can determine his potential success and failures in the relationship. Furthermore, a man that works hard to improve his performances in each element within clusters would accomplish great successes in meeting the needs of a woman. Men and women can use the Cluster Dynamic Metrics to appraise their performance in relation to meeting the preferences that strengths their relationship. Interestingly, people that are open-minded but not yet dating and those already in a relationship may help each other with the scoring process. They may also take turns to score for each other to identify misconceptions they hold. Furthermore, the scoring will help them to undertake an analysis to gauge the improvements required for the level of compromise they could achieve in their relationship. When a couple decides to use the framework together, the scores they achieve form the basis for discussion to improve elements that can cement their relationship. Some people may want to learn more about the framework to become skilled at the analysis. As such, the next topic explains how the advanced evaluation stage comprising of more calculations can be tackled.

Advance Cluster Dynamics

The Advanced Cluster Dynamics Metrics (ACDM) is a performance metrics comprising of a statistical process that needs tackling beyond the reading of this book. The statistical process involves a digitalised presentation using honestly scored and computed data to achieve accurate and detailed results. The results are also presented in a clear and detailed report for individuals seeking clarification over their performance to attain a fulfilling relationship. People are generally concerned with performance issues because they determine one's level of achievement in making the other happy. Hence, the tool provides a more detailed process that can be undertaken meticulously using rigorous calculations. The calculations are translated into a report containing information and percentage figures to illustrate and compare performance levels. The calculations are digitally computed and can be commenced through an online course on **Advanced Compatibility course**. The training helps an individual or couples to learn about compatibility through personality traits and complementary values. The book supplies the Internet link for the course for those interested to learn about the tool in greater detail. The **Advanced Compatibility course** link is supplied at the end of this book. Anyone that takes the course will benefit a great deal from acquiring the knowledge and skills. People that have an excellent learning and application skill will grasp and apply the knowledge to become relationship advisors or would achieve everlasting and fulfilling relationships.

Initial Dates

There are benefits for a man that wants to understand and improve the level of his performance and compatibility in a relationship. The man could achieve benefits after improving the quality of his relationship to attain happiness, mental health, companionship and tranquillity. A man should be overjoyed when he knows that he can achieve a fulfilling relationship with a woman he loves. More so, when a man acquires skills to improve compatibility on traits and performance in respect of complementary values, he could achieve the level of happiness. Mostly, the fulfilment that a man could achieve would be consistent with his scores from the Personality Identifier and Cluster Dynamics Matrices. The aggregate scores attained by a man from the tools are more meaningful when evaluated or compared against the values of prospective or a current lover. The man's aggregate scores would also help him to develop mental strength on issues relating to a romantic affair. When a male identifies his shortcomings, he needs to face reality with determination to gain strength. It may seem that women are intolerant of a man's deficiencies. In reality, it takes a compatible woman or one with the ability to tolerate differences to be considerate. More so, it takes a woman with complementary values that are nearly aligned with the performance demonstrated by the dominant clusters to be able to tolerate some deficiencies in a man.

Therefore, if a man possesses qualities that are different to the woman's and performs poorly on her values, there are more chances that conflicts may become daunting. However, a man capable of adjusting or refining his deficiencies would improve the quality of his relationship. Some men may not make effort to apply creativity, patience and diligence to become effective at evaluating a woman's personality traits and complementary values. However, a person cannot become effective without having mastered or gained knowledge from the CDM and PIM tools. The CDM and PIM tools enable a man to facilitate his understanding of compatibility and complementary values. A person can demonstrate effectiveness in applying the matrices if he could achieve positivity in his relationship with a willing partner. Sometimes a person can quickly identify progress from the discussion he holds with a potential suitor in the initial dating days.

While it might not be a good practise to be judgemental, sometimes it is helpful to align a gut feeling with the tools to get a result based on suitability. A man might be correct to base his assumptions on intuition. Sometimes a dude may quickly surmise a woman's traits and gets lucky at quickly preventing a potentially disappointing relationship. Nevertheless, there are occasions when a man might get confused with the correct position of the woman's personality traits or complementary values. It requires the man to be committed to finding the true position and prove the correct traits and values of the woman.

When a man identifies that it is difficult to take an assessment of values and traits on a specific woman, he should investigate where the challenge lies. Some very clever or dishonest women can deliberately present a difficult or hidden personality. However, some man are not accustomed to honest, humble and innocent women so much that their personality traits and complementary values would confuse them. If an innocent woman mistakes the confusion for a bad vibe, it would cause her discomfort. Subsequently, the romantic relationship would be negatively impacted because the novelty feeling mostly associated with the beginning would be destroyed. Equally, when a clever or dishonest woman identifies a leeway from the confusion, she would enjoy dominating or deceiving the man. However, some clever women that are genuine may help the man by clarifying or leading on issues that benefit the success of the relationship. It takes a well-informed and highly skilled man to quickly and diligently deduce compatibility qualities and complementary values from either a conspicuous or a very devious woman. However, it may take few more dating opportunities to conclude that there is a possibility of sharing an everlasting and fulfilling romantic relationship. Nevertheless, the same man should realise that the woman would also be evaluating him in the same manner. Women would often want to identify if the man meets the expectations in line with her natural values that are also illustrated in the Cluster Dynamic Metrics (CDM).

A man needs to acquire excellent skills from using the tools that would help him to evaluate a potential suitor. The manner he conducts and evaluates his personal scores would help him to transfer the skills to deduce a woman's traits and complementary values through interacting with her. A man with excellent skills would use the scores from the Personality Identifier Metrics (PIM) and the CDM to effectively determine the possibility for achieving a fulfilling relationship with any specific woman. If a man lacks the skills to use the tools, there are chances that he may make catastrophic mistakes. A man might lose the best potential person if he hastily and wrongly judges the woman's personality traits. Most women are wrongly judged because they reveal their personalities more cautiously and gradually. In most cases, cautious women are more focused at reading the men while they control the projection of their image. Therefore, men have to be astute when leading conversations to get the best from women when they go on a date. In most instances, when a man leads a conversation with questions, a woman can deduce his personality qualities. The way a man response to questions gives the woman an insight on the values that he espouses. His responses usually expose to the female the exact clusters the man is bound to fulfil when they are fully into the relationship.

Most people sporadically consider certain elements without placing them into respective clusters. As a result, most women hover around the performance of elements that include generosity, politeness, romantic, and attentiveness and humour. These elements are mostly considered on a first and second date before full clusters begin to be considered. However, if a man demonstrates some critical elements from each cluster on the initial days of dating, the woman would gradually become certain of the level of potentially for her to love him. Nonetheless, some women may expect high performance on her dominant cluster from the initial date although other clusters would remain relevant. A man that has prior knowledge or grasp of concepts may understand that a good perform on the dominant cluster would drive the woman's inspiration for love. A woman's most dominant cluster can be regarded as the code that drives or inspires her love. A woman's code or dominant cluster controls her ego and fascination. A man should also identify the origins of the principles behind one or more codes or dominant clusters. He is also supposed to perform better in the codes of the specific woman. When he identifies the principles behind one or more codes, it would help him to complement his performance with words that create a buzz for her. If a man knows the language that the woman appreciates, it means that their communication would be joyful and peaceful most of the time. People that enjoy their conversations are likely to experience a fulfilling relationship.

In most cases, a woman develops codes or dominant clusters from principles derived from bases such as religion, tradition or freethinking among others. Any person whose life is controlled by principles derives from the some roots is likely to behave in ways that relate to the most influential ones. It is important for a lad to develop an understanding of the principles behind the main code as it forms part of her thinking. It may not help to investigate about the principles of roots of the woman's code if the man performs poorly on the some cluster that he cannot improve as quickly as it might be needed. However, if the man understands and respects the principles that guide the woman's thinking, it would help him to try to be tolerant, patient and courteous, as long as he has hope to fulfil or improve.

Mostly, a man that uses the right words in communicating with a tolerant, patient and courteous woman can easily be understood and appreciated. The ability for a man to understand the principles and using the right language helps him to prevent unnecessary conflicts. When a man understands the principles of a code, it helps him to appreciate the challenging way a woman thinks and communicates. However, a woman that has more than one main code presents a challenging personality to some man. If a woman has more codes of similar value that are not linked, some men will get disoriented. It only works better when the codes of a woman are closely linked or the guy's strengths cover a wide spectrum of clusters. It is usually more beneficial for a man to possess strengths in many clusters because his performance would be considered versatile in fulfilling a woman's dreams.

Chapter 7

Dominant Clusters 1

The clusters in part 1 relate to the manner a man shows his merit in deserving a woman he wishes to attract. The merit clusters are mostly the initial values that attract a woman to a man before she could evaluate the emotional clusters to decide if the man is really worth loving. Since merit clusters relate to economic inspired performance, the rating of financial, visionary and the confidence cluster makes a man realise his status. If the woman's dominant cluster is rated very highly on any of the merit group, she might concentrate her decision on issues related to economics and certainty. A fairly high number of women possess a dominant cluster from the merit clusters. Most women consider the merit clusters as equally important as the emotional clusters. However, when two people have successful gone on few dating experiences, it usually means that the individuals are possibly on the right course of establishing a romantic relationship.

At this stage, a man would have to convince the woman that he understands her needs and will be able to satisfy them. Since many blokes do not perform very well on the merit clusters, society encourages them to concede when they lack the competence to satisfy a woman's code. A lad should make an informed decision based on his realistic understanding to communicate to the woman about these shortcomings. Lovers can succeed in running a fulfilling relationship if they apply decisions in earnest. If people ignore objectivity in favour of mere expediency, the future consequence might be regrettable. Men should realise that problems do not magically disappear without applying the best solutions. A man would need to get used to making tough decisions.

A. Financial Cluster

The financial cluster is one of the most important values for most people because it involves the survival of an individual and his dependants. Some societies usual judge the value of a man through the financial lens. A man can be judged favourably if he performs well or excellently on most of the elements within the financial cluster. This section serves to explain the definition of the cluster and its elements in relation to love. The perspective of a woman and society was used to define the expected performance of a man on each element. The value of a man is merited from the way he attracts and satisfies the desire of a woman to achieve a general accomplishment in living a decent life. The following elements are vital in enabling a man to understand the areas he needs to develop so that his lover and perhaps the society could judge his ability to manage a fulfilled relationship. Ladies use the financial cluster to understand if her future life with the man can be manageable with minimal financial problems.

Affordability

People generally define affordability according to the quality of life they lead or what they desire their life to represent. Therefore, when people comment on affordability of a man, they relate his expenditure to economic environment and other comparative circumstances. In

74

particular, when some societies evaluate a man's ability to fend for his family, they consider his affordability on food, shelter, clothing and education for children. Societies that are more affluent believe that affordability defines a man's ability to provide a quality lifestyle. If a man fails to provide a luxurious lifestyle from food, shelter, clothing, holidays, education and other possessions, it means that his performance is poor. Therefore, when a woman tries to predict the man's financial performance, she takes into account her current or future desired lifestyle. Hence, a man should be able to prove to the woman if he is capable of meeting her needs. If the woman holds the financial code, she might emphasis on the affordability element. Nonetheless, the man has to analyse and establish if he could satisfy or match the level of taste preferred by the woman. Some women might hold a code from finance yet their quest for money may not rate above an average lifestyle. If a woman holds a financial code and still enjoys an average lifestyle, it means that she may not be obsessed with wealth but she could only fear to live in poverty.

Sustainability

Some ladies might have experienced individuals that spend lavishly to portray an image of being wealthy. Yet, the individuals would be overstretching their resources to make an impression to peers or a prospective lover. Therefore, some clever women would not be hoodwinked into believing a baseless impression likely to be created from stupidity. Sensible women are interested in seeing if the man is able to sustain the projected lifestyle for reasonably long time. A man that enjoys the benefits of a meticulously executed plan is usually able to maintain the income at a certain rate or level for a long time. The wealth of a man is not valued using the manner he spends his money. A wise woman might believe that a man possesses a reasonable financial strength only if he can prove viable sources that can sustain a favourable level of affordability for a long time. People realise that when a man creates a plan, his intention should be aimed at fending for his dependents for a long time. If his flow of income were to be affected, the impact to his sources should be caused by changes that fall beyond his predictability and control. Hence, sustainability is a valuable element within the financial cluster that helps to attract and convince a woman that the man will effectively help in promoting a decent lifestyle for the family.

Competitiveness

Women weigh the competitiveness of men according to the opportunities they are offered by the society. If a man fails to attain average results, it means that he would be performing inadequately than the rest of his peer group. A person that does not achieve the average results in a society would mostly encounter deterioration in his standard of life. However, a man that achieves a higher level of affordability and sustainability than the average in his community could be regarded as competitive. A competitive man is one that works harder or has better opportunities than others in the same community. Naturally, a competitive man enjoys affordability and sustainability levels that are healthier than the average person in their economical environment. In addition, a man that satisfies the competitive element may withstand negative economical pressures that might impact on the livelihood of people in the relevant community.

Thus, if a man's competitiveness is above average, it means that he can fulfil the desires of a woman that judges him on the financial cluster.

Usability

Usability is an element that defines the management of finance that the man earns. A woman that expects a life long relationship can deduce from a specific guy if he is able to share and manage his finances. Few women can be duped into believing that senseless spending means that the man's affordability can be sustain forever. Similarly, a female would be hesitant to get involved with a fellow that shows stinginess. Ladies suspect that a tight-fisted man can make his family suffer while he enjoys seeing a fat balance in his account.

Equally, a man that uses this money without some level of answerability might be selfish. If a man uses his money without consultation on relevant issues means that he is irresponsible and unadvisable. Some man might have plausible reasons for avoiding consultation such as protecting the sanctity of his duties to the family. Some responsible people meet irresponsible partners and the burden of protection may fall on them to bring sanity to their financial affairs. Nonetheless, partners that do not work as a team face conflicts. The partners would encounter worse problems if they do not cooperate when trying to manage limited resources that fail to cover their basic needs. Lovers can resolve conflicts if they accept individuals' strength and weaknesses and agree on the best person to manage relevant components of finance. Hence, ladies evaluate a man's usability state to determine if sustainability and harmony can be achieved in the management of finance. If a lady has not clearly established usability before engagement or marriage, she might enter into marriage with uneasiness over finance.

Humbleness

Humbleness is an element that informs a woman that the man might afford and sustain a desired lifestyle and remains humble. A lad that achieves an above average level of wealth might choose to be inaccessible to loved ones because of pride. Similarly, some guys might become frustrated and angry because of poverty. When some lads live with frustration and anger, they become abusive to people around them. As a result, ladies are afraid of man that harm loved ones when their financial situation changes. The humbleness element shows that income at any level can affect the happiness of people in a relationship. Some women would never choose to suffer abuse at the hands of a wealthy man because of the luxurious life she could lead if married to him.

B. Visionary Cluster

The visionary cluster has overly been exhausted in the book because many women own it as their code or a dominant preference. In this section, the visionary cluster has been written for purposes of giving brief definitions of the individual elements that make up the cluster. The visionary cluster is one that relates to a man's effort towards making a life meaningful through his contribution to the development of his economic, political and social life. In other words, the visionary cluster in some senses would

78

define a man's current or potential influence within his home, community or society. The elements that define the visionary cluster include being a planner, strategic, leading, organised and ambition.

Planner

Women love a man that plans his life in a purposeful way for the benefit his family and the society at large. Women prefer to be part to a life that has a logical plan that determines the direction of future life. Generally ladies do not like to contribute their strength to a meaningless life because they value the welfare of their future children. As a result, the planner quality is an important element within the visionary cluster that men have to fulfil.

Strategic

The strategic element is the most difficult one as it determines the intelligence of a man in implementing the goals that have been planned. Men that plan and implement their goals in a strategic manner attract admiration from knowledgeable women. If life were lived without understanding various challenges, it would be difficult for anyone to navigate creatively to achieve the goals. Hence some women realise that a strategic man often finds ways to survive in very difficult circumstances. As such, a man that shows high performance in the cluster would be achieving greatly on the strategic element.

Leading

Women know that when planning, strategizing and organising life for now and the future, the best can be achieved if a person effectively uses leadership qualities. Furthermore, several women arguably state that they are attracted to men with a vibe of power. As such, a man capable of leading would possess many qualities such as confidence, charisma and people's skills.

Organised

The element of being organised has been placed separately because of its important role within other elements of the visionary cluster. A man that appears organised is one that a woman can judge as being less haphazard on a plan. It means that a man would lead and implement his plan meticulously through a strategy. Men that are organised can trace and verify their progress to identify threats, weakness, opportunities and strengths. Equally when a man is organised, he would drive his plan to follow general timeframes that might be flexible depending on the critical and other factors that have been considered. Women need a person whose life journey can be easy to understand. If a person is not organised, he can be difficult to comprehend and that may give a sinister man an opportunity to deceive a woman on a number of things that impact the relationship. The organised element is one that men need to perform very well if they could impress an equally organised person. The visionary cluster would not be complete without the organisation that supports other elements to become overwhelmingly more distinct.

Ambitious

Generally, many women have numerous ways to identify if a man is ambitious. Ambition is an element that complements other components of the visionary cluster. Females that possess the visionary code are able to detect if the man has a hunger for development or success. A man cannot work hard to achieve success or development if he lacks ambition. It is not possible for any person to create a plan without an idea that can be implemented to achieve noble goals. It is a prerequisite for every man to be ambitious in life so that it could propel his critical and strategic thinking. Hence, any bloke that can think strategically would mostly produce and dedicate to a workable plan. A plan has a high chance of succeeding if the implementation is organised through quality leadership. Each ambitious person aims to achieve the goals that he sets after coming up with an idea. As such, a man that has an ambition can be identified through his determination to create the best ideas. Furthermore, a man would work hard towards meeting the objectives of his ideas despite facing obstacles along the implementation process. Women that possess the visionary code are often put off by less ambitious man.

Ladies that are attracted to ambitious men feel inspired when they are around them. The males may not speak of their ambitions more often but the ladies would usually find it easy to deduce the element from general talk, lifestyle, endeavours, achievements and connections. In particular, some women that hold the visionary code are often hardworking and inspiring in their own right. Thus, the women that possess the visionary code are very good at spotting from potential lovers their level of hunger for success or development. A man with a desire to do better in life could improve his performance through acquiring or enhancing his knowledge and skills. When a person decides to enhance his knowledge and skills, he aims to become better in his efforts. Equally, if he were to encounter failure, his knowledge and skills would be helpful in minimising the impact. It is also helpful for a man to be surrounded by people with similar disposition for development or success for the good of the society. Some women recognise that a man that interacts with hard working colleagues benefits from the network in many ways. Hence, ladies are able to identify a visionary man from the quality of his connections among others.

C. Confidence Cluster

Women are drawn to men that are confident because they can be inspiring and assuring. Females are well aware that most confident men are likely to know what they want today and in future. Women love certainty in their lives and if the man shows no sign of assurance, the experience in the relationship would markedly seem dull and directionless. Therefore the confidence cluster is more defined when the following elements such as excitable, eloquence, trustworthy, self-aware and tidy are identified within experience of a relationship.

Excitable

If a man does not show any excitement in his relationship with a woman, she would not be sure if he is interested. In addition, a man that lacks enthusiasm does not inspire a woman and he would never be fun to be around. Therefore, a man that cannot be excitable would not bring fun, easiness and interest. As such, the man would make the woman feel as if her life has become drab. Women are aware of the need to take life seriously in other circumstances, but if it is a persistent feature, it means he will drag the woman in a perpetual state of dullness. Most ladies love a life with purpose, hope and happiness. If a man lacks the zeal that would be evidenced by a bit of impulsiveness, most females would not feel a connection or liveliness. Therefore, excitability is one form of expression that defines confidence in the experiences that a woman encounters with a man. A man has an obligation to make every experience precious for him and his lover. The lad would feel animated if the female also gives the same vibe. Hence, relationships are more exciting and appreciated if they are made lively.

Eloquence

There is no better way for a woman to feel inspired than when she meets a man that can express his aspirations, love and commitments with clarity, certainty and brilliance. A bloke may have excellent plan in his life but if he cannot express it, it is meaningless to most ladies. A lad may have deep feelings for a woman but if his eloquence is poor, she may not feel the emotion. Likewise, a guy may value life in an inspirational way but if his eloquence is lacking, the female may not connect with him. Eloquence is of great value to any type of connection and women in general have a weakness for it. Some women are not able to identify any element that might match the magic of eloquence that defines confidence. A person that can be considered as eloquent is not usually misunderstood because of a person centred approach that helps to create a suitable way to provide clarity. Nonetheless, there are bad people that take advantage of others with their eloquence to convince them for selfish reasons. Hence, some women are sceptical and fearful of men that use eloquence to con victims. It is sometimes very difficult to gain the trust of a woman that might be well versed with the art of eloquent conmen. However, men need to perform excellently on the eloquence element that adds a significant value to the confidence cluster.

Trustworthy

Most women are drawn to men that demonstrate an aura of trustworthiness from the first time they meet. According to some women, they feel that trustworthy men are few because they rarely come across them. As a result, most women would feel blessed if they could find someone trustworthy. It takes a long time for a woman to become completely certain that the man is trustworthy. However, in the preliminary stages of a relationship, a guy has an obligation to show his potential suitor that he is trustworthy. It is not convincing to show the element of trustworthy with hesitation. Therefore, the lad can only indicate the element of trustworthiness with certainty. A confident man can demonstrate his integrity in more creative ways to become more appealing to a woman. Ladies do not judge trustworthiness from expressed words that directly sound like a self-recommendation or arrogance. Hence, women prefer to derive the element of trustworthiness from actions and discussions that they would hold a long dating period.

Self-aware

Self-aware is an element that helps a woman to feel that the man consciously understands his strength and weakness. Women feel that a man that shows that he is self-ware can expose his level of confidence. A self-aware person is usually humble and respectful yet confident and driven. If a person is obsessed with his abilities, appearances and his needs, he ceases to be self-ware but arrogant. Self-awareness should be a controlled element of consciousness that makes a woman be drawn to a man. When a bloke is arrogance, it becomes hard to trust such a person because he may not embrace any regard for another human being. Thus, a person who is self-aware can easily be identified because he would be found being comfortable in the way he behaviours. People that are not self-ware may appear arrogant or would come across as liars.

Tidy

When a man that looks tidy in his manner of dressing and acting would mostly come across as confident. Tidiness is an element of confidence because it purifies all the elements to present clarity and smoothness to a potential lover. Women are attracted to some level of tidiness within all elements of the confidence cluster. Some people may assume that tidiness is similar to being organised but a disorganised person my also be tidy. Therefore, tidiness cannot be defined without any of the elements within the confidence cluster. Since confidence is defined from the action, appearance and expression, if any of the factors lack tidiness, a man would seem confused or untrustworthy.

Chapter 8

Dominant Clusters 2

The clusters in the part 2 are emotion based and they indicate the ability for a man to develop meaningful connection with a woman. Hence the emotional clusters allow a woman to observe the manner a man expresses or demonstrates his love. A man has to succeed in drawing a woman's attention to achieve emotional connection through the acts that help him to demonstrate his love. A woman's code or dominant cluster is an inscription that defines her ego and cannot easily be erased unless she feels read to adjust it. Some selfless women know that they would be a clash of personalities when they encounter men that exhibit selfish characteristics. It is common knowledge among females that a clash of personalities often results in her experiencing a terrible romantic life. Therefore, women are mostly keener than men but sometimes they equally fail to grow the relationship to become mature and enjoyable. Some self-destructing women also know that there is value in an open communication, as it helps to resolve misunderstandings and improves commitment matters. However, people fail to admit that each dating experience reaches a stage where parties to the relationship must become more frank with each other to enable reaching a compromise for the sake of resolving problems. Some progressive women feel that certain men are reluctant to discuss commitment among other importance issues in a relationship.

Men equally need to recognise and subscribe to the view that when extreme tendencies are challenged, not only would clarity be achieved, but the relationship should also be allowed continue growing. When people learn to resolve matters at the dating stage, it usually helps to adjust the egos of both individuals in the relationship. The dating stage reveals to individuals that it is an unhealthy imbalance if only one individual makes the enormous effort to please the other. However, men should appreciate that they would never succeed in forcing a woman to alter her code or dominant cluster. His focus should be targeted at making sure that he works hard to satisfy her needs or being honest to her that he would not succeed in making her happy if adjustments from his side are to painful and impossible. If a man continues with the relationship without achieving meaningful compromises on challenging elements from specific clusters, he is likely to face endless relationship problems. At most, if the man appears to be confused about the code or dominant cluster of the woman, it may cause him to wrongly think that she holds jumbled mannerisms. Yet in most cases, the man may lack the required knowledge about her expectations. In some respects, the woman might be genuinely projecting confusing characteristics that the man fails to understand.

There are some women that exhibit incoherent personalities that are compounded by the difficulty to express their preferences. A person that was socialised from a combination of many conflicting ideologies such as liberalism or carefree attitude, cultural and religious beliefs would mostly display disjointed flow of values and personalities. Few men might manage to deduce ways to understand some common preferences from women that exhibit incoherent personalities. A small number of men usually focus on deducing some relevant preferences from the women's reaction to expressions, behaviours, comments and discussions. The reactions might be rude, dismissive, demeaning, humorous, revengeful or controlled depending on the issue under discussion. A clever man establishes a pattern from a series of reactions to evaluate compatibility and his performance on the complimentary values. Every male has an equal responsibility to evaluate and eliminate possible actions or traits that are likely to create antagonism in his relationship. It is vital for every man to predict the possibility of enjoying harmony in his romantic journey with the woman he would be dating. A lad has an equal duty to take action that promotes tranquillity in his future experience within the relationship. Once a man gets into a relationship with a female, he should realise that he assumes a share of responsibility to achieve success in the romantic affair.

In most cases, few women might temporarily suspend their codes for the sake of starting a relationship. However, when a woman suspends a code, it will eventually resurface to define her in a major way. Therefore, a gentleman should help the lady to promote her convictions as opposed to helping her to supress or destroy it. If the code is exhibited in an unhealthy manner, her commitment to permanent change helps the man to decide if the relationship is worth promoting. In cases where the code is exhibited in a healthy manner but the man cannot understand it, some males would partake with the woman in activities that shape her principles. There are numerous examples of successful relations that were improved when the man or woman joined the religion of the other. A lad would demonstrate nobility, love and optimism when he shows a mature level of commitment through joining a woman's church or beliefs to learn about her interests and aspirations. Progressive women value a man with unflinching commitment to fulfil her dreams. A man that inspires optimism and direction often wins trust, respect and certainty from a woman that loves decency, progress and tranquillity. Thus, the spirit of working as a team with respect and dignity helps to promote a rich and everlasting relationship. Men are able to achieve the best in each cluster if the women are supportive or behave in a manner that matches their expectations. Hence, it is important to provide a background of definitions associated with elements that make up each complete cluster.

D. *Emotional Intelligence Cluster*

It is important for men to use emotional intelligence when communicating or interacting with prospective or current lovers. Lads that use emotional intelligence enjoy so many benefits that also promote the strength and fulfilment of a relationship. Men need to realise that when emotional intelligence is applied, progressive women would feel motivated, appreciated, loved and treasured. Therefore, emotional intelligence is a form of self-control that can be experience in the manner a situation is handled to make an event pleasantly calm despite the potential for a hostile explosion. As such, when a man exercises emotional intelligence, he is likely to show tolerance and patience in the manner he would speak to his lover. A man cannot effectively practise emotional intelligence without the woman being able to detect sincerity in his approach. As such, a lad would not succeed in exercising emotional intelligence without assuming or sharing part of the responsibility. Equally, women would expect a guy to show some respect when interacting irrespective of misunderstandings. If a man would get a woman satisfied within the relationship, he needs to understand the elements that define emotional intelligence. More so, if the female holds emotional intelligence as the code or dominant cluster, the man has a duty to perform excellently on each of its elements to enjoy the relationship.

The emotional intelligence elements include politeness, attentiveness, humorous, forgiveness and accountability.

Polite

Politeness is one of the major elements that make emotional intelligence more definable and effective at promoting peace and harmony. At most, some women are drawn to men that are polite in their manner of solving problems and basically in the way they interact on a day-to-day basis. A polite man is mostly calm and level headed that deliberates on issues to find the best possible response. When a calm man finds solutions, he is usually considerate of the feelings of his team member. Hence, he gets consensus from bringing a lover on board during the decision process. However, the man would find the collective process becoming hard to pursue when the other part disregards him on matters that impact on their life. Most women know that men that are not polite are usually good at escalating tension or causing confusion in an abusive manner. Thus, a person that is polite is reassuring and does not like to be involved in violence or disrespectful disagreements.

Attentive

The behaviour of an attentive man is one of the most important elements that attract women. A person that listens to other people's views is normally able to weigh issues justly and responses in an amicable manner. If a man is able to be attentive to his lover, he usually uses emotional intelligence to solve issues. Most progressive women would work hard for a man to improve his attentiveness so that he could respect the views of others. A man that lacks attentiveness is often regarded as selfish, arrogant or ignorant. If there are no other insinuating circumstances, a guy that never pays any attention to women is more likely to be sexist, domineering, manipulative or contemptuous of other people's views. A man considered to be attentive is normally composed as he actively listens to the views of others in an engaging manner. Some men that are capable of exercising emotional intelligence are effective at communication. It can be reiterated that a man cannot be very effective at using emotional intelligence if he is not able to be attentive.

Humorous

There are times when a man would fail to place a distinction between humour and sarcasm. The people involved in a situation may fail to agree on a suitable inference relating to the contexts of the humour. If a guy applies humour without knowing the sensibility of the lover, he may offend her. Equally, when a woman employs humour in a way that offends a man, he needs to apply some elements of emotional intelligence to understand or control the feeling of dismay. If a man is aware of appropriate humour to use when he is with his lover, it helps him to prevent conflicts. Sometimes a person would need to know when a specific humour might be considered applicable. However, many women find that humour helps them to relax from possibly tense situations. Mostly, some women like a person that makes them laugh with humour. So men that are effective at using emotional intelligence apply humour to calm, lighten or charm a woman. Hence, humour is one of the most valued elements within the emotional intelligent cluster.

Forgiving

Forgiving is a valued element that takes strength for a man to extend to a lady. People rarely forgive before deliberating on the reasons an individual desires the act of kindness. It takes love, kindness and self-convincing for an individual to forgive another among other factors. Most people that are capable of forgiving use common sense to fight against deep emotions so as to liberate their souls from hurt. Of course, a person's level of hurt determines the amount of effort that one employs to forgive. Men that can control their pride are more capable of extending their forgiveness to women. Therefore, most sensible women love and respect a reasonable man for his ability to forgive. It takes a man with emotional intelligence to be able to find a justification to forgive. As such, it makes sense to describe a man as an emotional intelligent person if he can forgive. Forgiveness is an important element that can be classified as a major symbol of emotional intelligent. Nonetheless, it should also be acknowledged that a female would play a major role in making it easy for the man to forgive her. If she complicates the forgiving process, it means that the issue will remain without closure or would continue to intensify.

Accountable

Accountability is an act of accepting transparency in one's actions irrespective of the magnitude of bad result. Mostly, people love recognition of their accountability if they can be associated with the best results. When a man is accountable for his actions he does not shift blame to escape his deeds. It takes resolve for an individual to understand the importance or benefits of accountability. A man that applies his mind to become accountable usually is a very responsible individual. However, there are instances when strength is required to deal with a person that holds no regard for accountability. Some people want others to be accountable but never want the same for their bad actions. Most sensible women take pride in men that are accountable because they are also conscious of their responsibilities that benefits a collective union. The actions and conflicts behind accountability make it an important element of the emotional intelligence cluster.

E. Caring Cluster

Caring is a quality that most women love to experience in their relationship because of its therapeutic effect to the mind, body and soul. When one receives care, she would feel a sense of belonging, recognition and respect. Hence the caring cluster has elements that define it in a complementary fashion. Any woman that holds the caring code would never be happy in a relationship that lacks the majority of elements in the cluster. The caring cluster in made up of five elements, which include romantic, generous, reliable comforting and respect.

Romantic

A romantic man is one that is expressive of his love towards a woman and some woman would love to hear it expressed as many times as possible.

In particular, the women would love the expression of love to be repeated in many different ways so that they could feel the passion. The majority of ladies might be over the moon if love is expressed passionately through physical contact, materially and verbal expressions in public and in private. Some women that carry the caring code feel starved if they don't receive gifts or presents on major occasions such as birthdays, anniversaries, Valentine's Day, Christmas and Mothers Day. They would also feel honoured and loved if they were surprised with gifts at any other times. More so, the women would feel flattered if men buy them undergarments or jewelleries among other things of sentimental value. Thus, if a man meets a woman with a dominant caring cluster, his love can be highly appreciated if the romantic element is fulfilled. If he fails to effectively perform on the romantic element, he will frequently experience fractions within his relationship because the woman will feel undervalued.

Generous

A man needs to be generous in the way he deals with a lady to demonstrate his personality and the kind of life they would experience together. Generosity is very broad in its reach because it explains the kindness of an individual to people around and beyond. A generous man would know that if he is not giving, he could ignore the suffering or lack of prosperity of other people. A generous man gives with no intention for any reward or recognition. When giving, the main motivation would be to provide help rather than expecting something in return. Therefore, a person that draws inspiration to give from changing the lives of other people is genuinely generous. A generous man is one that shares his time, knowledge, resources and protection among others. If an individual is generous, he is likely to be a sympathetic and selfless person. Therefore, the generous element contributes massively in defining the caring cluster. Hence, women prefer to fall in love with a man that performs exceptional well on the generosity element. People that are generous inspire the idea of hope in a society. Their efforts are normally effective when they discourage manipulation, greediness and cruelty. Hence, when an equally generous woman meets the man, she anticipates achieving an everlasting and fulfilling relationship. If a woman holds the caring code, she would not compromise on the generous element. Hence, it was stated earlier that generous contributes significantly to the value of the cluster.

Reliable

The ideal achievement for couples at a dating stage is to connect emotionally and feel fulfilled from the love they relatively share in equal measure. Apparently, reliability is an element that most people take for granted. A question was asked to a sample of women in order to understand if they would manage to love a man who is not reliable. Some women provided an answer to the effect that it would be impossible to love an unreliable man. Other women stated that a man who is not reliable would make them live a frustrated life. It was then deduced from the answers that a man who is unreliable was difficult to love. Since love involves respect, treasure and a feeling of secure, it would be difficult to enjoy any of these if the man is not reliable. Therefore, a woman would want a man that she can count on when the need arises. It is not easy to predict a best effort from a reliable man. A reliable man is one that puts the best interest of the woman and other members of the society as a priority or above his personal needs. A reliable man is compassionate, dependable, honest, and helpful. People would expect a reliable man to perform tasks with commitment and selflessness at all times.

Comforting

People go through challenges in their personal, social and profession experiences to the extent that they end up facing distress or mental health challenges. A man may find that children, relatives, friends or a lover among many might be facing pain that emerges from different settings. It is important for a man to exercise kindness when approached by people that might be seeking help. However, women admire a man that voluntarily offers a comforting experience to people that may need it. A man with a kind heart is always willing to provide a comforting experience without being intrusive on people's privacy. A woman would be happy to be in love with a man that displays a compassionate heart. Hence, a woman would anticipate being comforted when the need arises. The comforting process can be direct or indirect depending on the position of privilege. They are many ways a man can render a comforting experience to a woman that does not require his kindness.

As such, a person's emotional intelligent may lead to a suitable comforting approach. Generally, a man should avoid demanding to know or forcing a solution to be accepted when the woman is being evasive with the issue impacting on her mood or mind. A woman would be pleased to know that the man can respect her reluctance to share the information until she is ready. Nonetheless, the woman would be flattered to know that the man was willing to devise an ingenious and meticulous way to comfort her. It is during tough moments in one's life when a lover's caring element can be visibly tested. The comforting element determines the extent to which one can be a strong supporting pillar to the loved one. Some women believe that several men can pretend to have a caring predisposition at the start of a relationship. However, the women allege that the truth about the nature of men would eventually be discovered immediate into the relationship. Furthermore, the women explain that in some instances they get to know the cold-heartedness of the men long after engagement or marriage.

Respecting

Females in general allege that they face a problem when it comes to being respected by men that are attached to them. Several ladies feel that the disrespect comes from the misogynist attitude of some males. People that debate the issue attribute males' lack of respect for ladies to religious, biological and traditional principles. As a result, men's performance on the caring cluster is considered relatively poor because of the respecting element. The respecting element diminishes the strengths of other elements within the caring cluster. Nonetheless, various societies tend to accept the lack of respect as the norm yet it is one of the crucial elements that define a person being humane. The difference in physical strength between women and men does not mean one is less a human than the other. Thus, it is vital for men to respect the dignity, privacy and emotional state of a lady, as he would expect her to equally perform on the caring cluster.

Romantic Perspectives 1

Chapter 9

Impactful Factors

People that are mature and have started to look forward to a future together should not go to the next step before examining issues that may affect their partnership. If a man would go ahead and marry or begin living with a woman, he needs to have developed a strategy to make his personal life fulfilling. A man that cannot find happiness will definitely make a woman miserable throughout their lives together. Since the visionary cluster determines the material forms of survival, it is pertinent in this book to provide more analysis and description on its impact to a relationship. Many societies encounter relationship challenges because of the failure to come to terms with various elements within the visionary cluster.

Hence, in writing this book there was a realisation that if the economic issue imbedded within the visionary cluster is not separately exhausted, some relationship challenges will be left vague. Therefore, the author examined the scope of the visionary cluster and identified issues that needed further expansion to prevent limiting the benefits from this book. While the economic status is appealing to several people before living with their lovers, the seriousness of the issues becomes challenging when they began sharing a home or life. The issue of finance is among the biggest factors responsible for conflicts that result in breaking relationships.

Visionary Impact

Women that possess a predisposition for a visionary cluster prefer men to demonstrate strength in their performance. In particular, the females expect men to present their plan to prove the authenticity of their direction, ambition knowledge and success. A vision is not presented in a blueprint but deduced from an observation or a general discussion held once or over a lengthy of time. Some visionary men may not realise that they are communicating their visionary plan because the information comes naturally or subconsciously. However, some women argue that men accuse them of lacking specific knowledge on processes of planning that help to attain the goals of a vision. Conversely, several men assume that women are not accustomed to their creative prowess. Hence, women allegedly state that men merely rely on promising a better future.

Some women further explain that they mostly derive information from conversations although they gradually unearth more evidence. Several other women argue that men are mistaken in their belief that they can convincingly make a promise for a better future to prove that he is a visionary. The women say that they do not entertain verbal explanations without milestone evidence that a man is visionary. The ladies require milestones that denote achievements in the form of progress on personal, professional or societal developments. Some women only measure success from the money or material achievements that they can identify. In general, women have an instinctive ability to identify if a man is evidently a visionary. However, as much as some men lie, there are some women that are unrealistic in expecting evidence of a very high quality to determine the strength of a man's visionary. Some women ignore the challenge that lads face in providing evidence of a very high quality to support their performance in the visionary cluster.

Many lads are constrained from providing the evidence by factors such as age, societal, educational, political and economic environment. The factors distort the lad's performance on the visionary cluster and they end up being portrayed as lazy, directionless, confused and less ambitious. Some men argue that women put unbearable pressure on them to achieve values that are beyond the reach of the majority at any given time. Nevertheless, some women express that their expectations are values that are ascribed by society and they are just the conduits of what is regarded as the norm. Women further explain that society is convincing because it provides examples for men that hold visionary evidence. The visionary evidence is paraded as the norm in many societies to the extent that everyone believes that every man is capable of creating one. Hence, the women believe that visionary evidence is not anything that any man could struggle to plan and execute. The ladies explained their understanding that some wealthy men may not be visionary as they might be born into a privileged life or made money through luck. Hence, women allege that some of the wealthy men without vision may easily become poor beyond recovery.

Men argue that some few people obliviously distort the meaning of the visionary domain by promoting the idealism of success and not the process. Men that hold respectable experience are normally ignored when they explain about the restraining factors that hardworking individuals navigate to succeed. Nevertheless, the desire for women to live a confortable life motivates some men to make an effort towards the visionary cluster. Some hardworking and visionary men understand the reality of 'no gain without pain'. Hence, some women are attracted to individuals that are never deterred by any hindrances from trying to improve the society or change their fortunes. Nevertheless, few men perform well on the visionary cluster because they fear the impact of financial risks. Since the process of implementing a vision usually takes longer than planned, men become adverse to visions that prolong their financial problems because some women that value instant cash will estrange them. Men understand that financial problems limit their ability to reach and be accepted by some desired women. Some women declare that they will never fall in love with a man who is broke. Some women would not care if the men's disposable income were restricted due to some investments. The few ladies assume that the bloke is stingy or poverty-stricken. Hence, several men realise that if their poor economic status were noticed at the starting point of a relationship, it may prevent the affair from taking off.

A handful of women understand that some men respect them for accommodating the males' visionary prowess than financial wealth. The type of women know that if the lads feel appreciated and supported, it may unleash confidence, high performance and possibly excellent results. Therefore, a man can develop an ability to assess decent qualities from a woman if he gains skills from the CDM tool. A man that lacks tolerance and patience would dispel or ill-treat a woman with excellent and admirable qualities. Some men can thrive in a relationship if they find women who do not hold the dominant visionary code. Women that do not possess a dominant visionary code may only be concerned about other issues that do not relate to money, power or personal success.

Nevertheless, every gentleman equally owes his lover an honest discussion on the visionary context to achieve consensus on the best way to survive. If a man fails to address the visionary issue with a woman who is fastidious on the subject, the issue will cause endless misunderstandings or permanent damage to the relationship. Some people are not familiar with the visionary cluster and their interpretation of it would be described from an economic perspective. People that believe in the economic perspective understand that a man's poor economic circumstance would mostly impede the success of a relationship.

Economic Impact

Arguably, women are expected to value the thoughtfulness or in some cases the generosity that men may extend when involved in a romantic relationship. There is always a debate from the question relating to the actions of reasonable men and women. It is expressed that women are considerate and can control their level of expectation from their lovers. It is argued that the realistic anticipation of women in expressing a desire for thoughtfulness from men should be based on many factors. It is assumed that woman that are rational consider the impression they project in anticipation for thoughtfulness from men they would be dating. Hence, women that are rational are not overly demanding in their anticipation from men's thoughtfulness or kindness. Women value a man's financial status from his lifestyle and commitments versus the economic environment. Most women are aware that bad men may use money as a destructive force to cheapen their value. Some females became dispirited after experiencing men that use their financial power to lure them for their own gratification. When a wealthy lad feels he wants to jilt the lady,

104

he will make sure that he abused or degraded her first. Thereafter, the man would use his plausibly stupid reason to justify his twisted psyche for jilting the lady. Some dudes take advantage of women because of a limited number of men that provide them a luxurious life.

At the same time, there are too many women that want a man with a better economic status. As a result, every woman that endures abuse by holding on to a man with economical strength does so to fulfil her code or ego. As such, most women wonder if the men realise how abusive behaviour debases their dignity. In particular, women realise that perverted wealthy men target powerless young ladies because of their gullibility and lack of life experience. Nonetheless, the young ladies are pleased with the treatment because of the material benefits they receive from men. Mostly, the ladies argue that apart from the benefits that temporarily take them out of poverty, the experience teaches them about life. The young females justify their decisions by explaining that when the relationships end, they would still be very young but a bit wiser to start fulfilling relationships with improved wisdom. However, women of wisdom always encourage society to protect and prevent younger females from blindly getting into relationships that would suddenly be terminated at the detriment of an emotional damage. The society has since time immemorial been trying to encourage financially privileged men to take responsibility to promote decency by desisting from damaging the innocence of disadvantaged young women. The argument is considered stronger because an emotionally damaged woman would not effectively conduct her role of being a pillar to the community with virtue that promotes stability.

Men do not realise that woman build communities through raising children and integrating them into the society. As such, the abuse of women by men creates a society of ladies that are angry, distressed, remorseful and distrustful. When some of the women become mothers, they are likely to remain emotionally distressed because of the perception of an unjust society. If only some men would realise, they would discourage others from being negative contributors so that they prevent tumultuous situations in some communities. Mostly, the perverted and distrustful men remain in privileged society while they are oblivious of their contributions to problems in mainly poor communities. Hence, progressive young women prefer relatively genuine and hardworking young men that believe in achieving milestones gradually and incrementally for long-term purposes. The young men realise that it takes long and hard work to achieve high salaries or income and to acquire assets of high value. Hence, the young and ambitious men are commonly advised to be patient and to look for suitable women that are not inclined to immediate success. However, money can be the most problematic item in a relationship, as some men believe spending excessively on a woman could be the only way to demonstrate reliability and generosity. Ordinarily, most women believe that success can be validated through economical strength and stability.

Therefore, some relatively shortsighted women believe that men that lack financial resources as evidence of achievements cannot claim to have any future plans that may succeed. Hence, the myopic minds held by some members of the society lead to a socialisation of restricted minds. Men should be aware of few women that assume the volume and quality of gifts indicate the wealth of a man. It is commonly known that some men lead extravagant lifestyles from illegal proceeds. The men portray economical strength from the silhouette of illegal proceeds. However, some women do not realise that illegal proceeds cause most men to spend extravagantly to impress them. A few good lads with limited resources also emulate or attempt to compete with guys that extravagantly spend illegal money to lure some greedy females. The good lads do not realise that they will be competing with men that spend illegal proceeds recklessly because of the risk of saving or using it constructively. If the men use illegal proceeds wisely, it would eventually be confiscated when they get arrested. The men know that they will be arrested at some point so they will spend the illegal proceeds before the inevitable happens.

However, few women realise that after being overwhelmed with gifts, their appetite for more increases. When the spoiled women become accustomed to the greedy world beyond redemption, the habit becomes detrimental to their persona and everyone around them. As a result, most of the women become disrespectful to guys that live a normal life, who are apparently in the majority. The behaviour of greedy women will become worse than the financially illiterate and generally ignorant ladies that abuse their boyfriends because they offer too limited resources when they receive help. It is evident that men and women need to be realistic about finance if they want to enjoy their relationships. If they are not realistic, at most they will never enjoy a peaceful relationship. More so, they will eventual cause their lives to become perpetually miserable forever.

Chapter 10

Proposing Phase

Women understand that generally men are mostly hesitant to commit to marriage despite entertaining the idea. Likewise, some men believe that more women are too keen to get married much quicker. However, some women may openly express to men their eagerness to get married sooner. Originally, biological factors created a strong desire for women to enter into a stable marriage to bear children at a relevant age. The biological factor instinctively leads women to realise the health benefits for a mother to give birth while still relatively young and strong. Women are generally aware of the impact of the biological factor if they give birth after the age 40 years. Women are aware of medical researches that identified the increased health risks for the child when a woman gives birth at age 40 years or older. Nevertheless, some societies became too ignorant and began to practice early marriage at the detriment of weak and immature girls. The societies' ignorance ware perpetuated as traditional and religious practices. However, most societies have always regarded marriages as a milestone and a symbol of pride in the life of a mature woman. In modern and affluent societies, they commonly believe that marriage is regarded as an important form of acquiring a close lifetime companion. Therefore, some men need to understand the value of marriage from the perspective of women.

Marriage does not mean the same to different women but the bottom line remains that it is a great life milestone for others. Some women believe that marriage is one of the most revered statuses that contribute to the societal character in the life of human beings. Hence, people aspire for a happy marriage so that they contribute one of the joyful characters to a society. Nonetheless, the history of marriage indicates that not all women aspire for it. The women might only want to associate with a man for love, companionship, childbearing and raising children outside what a few call 'an over burdensome shackle' which describes the perception of marriage. People that characterise marriage as a shackle may choose to stay out of it because of personal reasons possibly relating to a natural inclination and direct or indirect distressing experiences. However, a man that believes in the woman he loves might want to take advanced steps to demonstrate the growth level of their relationship. A man might take further steps after determining the suitability of a woman that matches his personality traits and marriage ambition. More so, when a man strongly believes that he can satisfy the complementary needs of the woman without abnormal stress, he would be enthusiastic to take a further step in their relationship. When a man establishes a convergence of traits and ambitions, he may logically incline himself to undertake an action towards fulfilling his and the woman's dreams. The most logical and exhilarating step for both persons would be, 'Will you marry me!' proposal.

However, people may be bound by aspirations and beliefs from personal, family, religion, culture and tradition to determine an appropriate root towards marriage. If love and understanding are reciprocal in almost equal measure, most disruptive challenges to the prospect of marriage might easily be defeated. Importantly, a man needs to help a woman to believe and define their scent of love so that she could values the humility and greatness of their future. A marriage proposal indicates the most important and honourable step in a relationship before the actual marriage. If extended to the right person who feels the love, honesty and chemistry, the man would be confident of a happier marriage. A man has to be convinced that he is doing the right thing to prevent making the woman miserable because of his regrets. Generally, if a man correctly interprets preferred characteristics, he would only fail to sustain them by becoming complacent or when events in his life take an uncontrollable turn. When a woman reacts negatively to complacence or mishaps, he should not be surprised unless he has just been naïve. However, when a man continues to develop a romantic relationship, he should question his sincerity or naivety. A man does not need to transfer his frustrations onto a woman after continuing with a relationship he knew lacked compatibility. Equally, a man would need to control his frustrations after continuing a relationship with a woman he could not satisfy her complementary preferences.

A woman's dominant preferences usually signal future challenges if a man has related deficiencies. Some man might naively take advance steps with a woman he shares incompatible qualities because of his fixation over her immensurable beauty. A man needs to be aware of a woman's dominant preference so that he evaluates to find if it aligns or measures to his dignity. If the dominant preference does not align with his dignity, his next question should relate to his ability to devise means to cope with possible challenges. It has to be appreciated that women also cope with many challenges from men's shortcomings. Mostly, women can begin to deduce men's shortcomings from the start of a relationship. As such, women might choose to continue with a man that lacks compatible qualities due to love, gullibility or in few cases greed. Nevertheless, men must appreciate their choices when they knowingly fall for women that would potentially be distressing in future. Some women that are ambitious need men that support and understand them. Sometimes a man's ambition may not be at par with his woman and he needs to know if she would appreciates him. Men that feel comfortable with ancient based ideas from tradition and religion may not cope with a modern and driven woman. Most highly driven women work relentlessly towards achieving professional or entrepreneurial success. However, most men should make sure that they do not hoodwink a woman into marriage. The woman would end up being displeased with the way she was driven into marriage. Some women detest and will never forgive a man that lies to win over her affection. Nonetheless, few women are forgiving and would rather concentrate on improving or adjusting to become content with her new life.

Compromising Theory

A compromise theory indicates the level of distance from which each person needs to travel to narrow the gap. The theory helps people in a relationship to find common grounds on a particular issue. A compromise does not necessarily mean that the other would grudgingly accept a position without accepting or giving the other a chance to try and make something work. The figure 4 provides a simple or elementary framework that illustrates the possibility for individuals to reach a compromise.

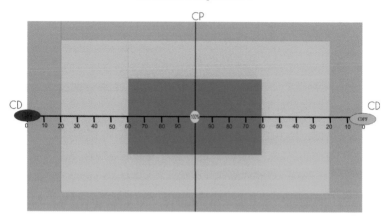

Figure: 4 Comprometre

The above Comprometre is a simple framework that was derived from the advance concept that explains the manner a compromise can be reached. The horizontal line shows the compromising distance (CD) that an individual has to travel from the starting position to reach the centre of agreement. The centre marked by 100% is the compromising point that represents an ideal point that brings the best win-win situation. When the issue is outlined, the parties to the discussion each move from the left Compromising Distance Point for Male (CDPM) and the right Compromising Distance Point for female (CDPF) to take their initial preferred positions. The one that starts from a far away point might have to work harder to come closer to 100% compromising point. Once two parties reach a 60% and above points each, it means that they are reaching a reasonable point where if they do not attain a 100% position, one part may have to try the better point with a higher score and if it fails, another's alternative might be adopted to achieve a better result. However, people might choose a lesser score first to prove a point before reverting to the best score that offers a better solution. A total compromise of 100% can be accomplished when there is no final difference in opinion. As such, when people adopt a 100% point, it means that they would have adopted an absolute congruous position that represents a win-win decision.

Sexual Intimacy

The issue of sex is something that plays in people's minds more than what might be considered necessary. Sex is an issue that goes with consent as it follows a compromise between two people. Therefore, sex is something that people engage in accordance to their dictates. In some cases, people prefer to follow the directives of their religion, culture and beliefs. People assume that the dynamics leading to engaging in sex should follow a universal pattern. The only universal part to sex is consent, which becomes the final and substantive element to its engagement. The rules regarding stages of a relationship that leads to sex are often regarded as subjective and relative to different situations. In some cultures, a man can only marry a virgin and they cannot compromise for any other reason. Men and women in general agree and uphold the cultural principle in that community. However, few people that might violate the principle may face punishment. Some societies do not restrict the choices of people when it comes to sex. Apart from promoting consent, some societies are not fixated at judging people despite encouraging social values, morals and decency. Therefore, men should understand and value the beliefs of a society and women's personal interests. Equally, men should express their interest relating to sex without necessarily being hasty to engage. Most women value a relationship that begins on a solid foundation of respect, emotional and physical connection. Importantly, men that are dating women should realise that sexual chemistry is a valuable component that might develop gradually.

There are insinuating factors that determine when to begin engaging in sex after starting a relationship. Many relationship experts have recommended a 3 months rule to begin engaging in sex. Men have a duty to identify a woman's preference and to communicate their interests so that he reaches an understanding or compromise with the woman. A man needs to effectively investigate a woman's beliefs relating to sex. It is more ideal for a man to begin communicating by giving sexual teasers in a restrained manner within 2 months of starting the relationship. In a modern society, sexual health is a major conversation that men need to take their part in introducing. When a man begins giving teasers, sexual health should be part of the discussion. The conversation process needs to be gradual and subtly in the initial stages to allow the other part to be comfortable and openly contribute to the discussion. While some people quickly get the gist and immediately contribute to the discussion, others would need clarification on the motivation behind sexual health among other related topics. It is important to use emotional intelligence in relaying the motivation that triggered the subject. The most sincere approach for a man is provided in the essence of the subject the need for responsibility, love, attraction and respect. It is fair to recognise that people do not always engage the same decision making processes and equally, solutions are often different.

Hence, some people do not begin with emphasis on the intention to engage in the sexual practice. The subject on sex for some is based on how they relate to its value because of abstinence reasons relating to celibacy, restricting until marriage or seeking commitment. As such, men will realise that the subject of sex will gradually increase in prominence at the dictates of the growth stages of the relationship. The growth process of a relationship helps to shape a couple's unique persona that defines their exclusive bond. Hence, a couple's relationship dynamics may supersede a recommended period to begin engaging in sex. Some people develop a unique chemistry that defies logical sense and can only be described by the two people. However, most women try to avoid any unusual rush to preserve their dignity and prevent heartbreak. Research identified that sexual chemistry provides the mostly satisfying feeling that can be experienced without putting too much effort. Nevertheless, the majority of people also excel when they openly communicate their commitment, shortcomings and desires to achieve sexual growth in their relationship. Therefore, it is clear for most men that openness, respect, commitment, understanding and compromise are essential to a satisfying sexual experience in a relationship.

Commentary

A man embarks of a long journey to seek love from a woman that he intends to love forever. His journey would be complicated if the man fails to be realistic about the behaviour of people and the environment that shape them. If a man fails to be realistic, he would possible face challenges to accept that he can never control anything in his life. It is his duty to adjust and compromise so that when he is luck to meet a reasonable people, they would value each other in relatively similar way. Therefore, each man should begin a journey of love with an open mind but without preparing to undergo a complete change to some values that define him. A person's values would be influenced for a complete change if he meets a person that has totally different perspectives to his own. His attempt to change might equally be painful because both individuals would be moving from very wide distances to narrow the gap in order to compromise. However, if the tools in this book were used earnestly and correctly, people would choose each other after a careful analysis.

It would also mean that each person would find it easier to narrow the gap of differences to reach a compromise because the initial distances would be shorter for both individuals. As a result, the pain of change would not be felt because it would not alter each individual's character. The Personality Identifier and the Cluster Dynamic Matrices would help a man to realise the potential of achieving a fulfilling relationship that would lead him to propose a woman for marriage. Thus, this book will be a benefit to any man that intents to improve his chances of finding a woman he would want to marry and be happy forever if he and his woman put a deserving effort to the dynamics in their lives. This book is followed by a part 2 that provides some incite into ways that can potentially improve harmony and love in marriage to couples that are determined to live a fulfilling and everlasting marriages. Furthermore, the 2 books are complemented by some courses that can be undertaken online to understand the tools that are used to improve compatibility and congruence on preferences and performances.

Know how to love her

Understanding and appreciating her, she will blossom with Love

Loving and committing to her, she will feel treasured

Respect would be her value to cherish

If valued, she senses the deepest love

Deeply indeed, her warm embrace would show her love

Smiles galore, she glows with warmth

Grace in her heart, the joy fills her emptiness

Her embrace is the fruit of effort

The honour received would equally be returned

The growth of love follows the honour

Cherished in return, the best is appreciated

Increase her worthiness, not her insecurity

Promote her code, not your dictates

Build no selfishness, but the power of devotedness

With inspiring self-love, confidence might breed certainty

As assured love inspires a great future

Compatibility, the compromise ball

Compromise comes from the fruit of knowledge

Enhancing the compromising skill shows the desire

If fulfilled, compatibility continues to flourish

Compatibility and stability, the ball of love

Resist ignorance for love to blossom

Achieve tenderness for happiness to be the glory

Frameworks & Courses

1. Personality Identifier Metrics

Figure: 1 on page 12

Advanced Metrics course: www.profca.co.uk/training/social

2. Due Diligence System

Figure: 2 on page 41

Metrics course: www.profca.co.uk/training/social

3. Cluster Dynamics Metrics

Figure: 3 on page 62

Advanced Metrics course: www.profca.co.uk/training/social

4. Compromise Theory

Figure: 4 on page 112

Advanced Metrics course: www.profca.co.uk/training/social

Contact

Website: www.profca.co.uk/training/social

Email: training@profca.co.uk

Email: enquiry@profca.co.uk

Email: lifecoaching@profca.co.uk

Bibliography

Antai, D. (2011), Controlling behaviour, power relations within intimate relationships and intimate partner physical and sexual violence against women in Nigeria, BMC Public Health, https://www.ncbi.nlm.nih.gov/pmc/articles/PMC3161889/, [Accessed: 19/06/19]

Hudson, M. (2019), What Is Social Media? https://www.thebalancesmb.com/what-is-social-media-2890301?utm_term=types+of+social+media&utm_content=p1-main-1-title&utm_medium=sem&utm_source=msn_s&utm_campaign=adid-0e8577d7-6aaf-4839-803a-b257a325a015-0-ab_mse_ocode-34462&ad=semD&an=msn_s&am=exact&q=types+of+social+media&o=34462&qsrc=999&l=sem&askid=0e8577d7-6aaf-4839-803a-b257a325a015-0-ab_mse, [Accessed: 19/06/19]

Hughes, K. (2014) Gender roles in the 19th century, https://www.bl.uk/romantics-and-victorians/articles/gender-roles-in-the-19th-century, [Accessed: 19/06/19]

James, K. and Resnick, P. J. (2007), Stalking intervention: Know the 5 stalker types, safety strategies for victims, Current Psychiatry. 6(5): 31-38

James, T. (2019) Online Dating Vs. Social Networking, https://itstillworks.com/online-dating-vs-social-networking-2858.html, [Accessed: 19/06/19]

Meyers, S. (2017) 5 Common Signs of Stalking Behaviour, https://www.eharmony.com/blog/signs-stalking-behavior/#.XQpt7i2ZNn0, [Accessed: 19/06/19]

Miller, L. (2012), Stalking: Patterns, motives, and intervention strategies, Aggression and Violent Behaviour, Volume 17, Issue 6, pp. 495-506, **https://doi.org/10.1016/j.avb.2012.07.001**

Odell A. (2012), 7 Ways Women Affect Male Behaviour, https://www.buzzfeed.com/amyodell/7-ways-women-affect-male-behavior, [Accessed: 19/06/19]

Radwan, M. F. (2017), What attracts men (the psychology of attraction of males), **https://www.2knowmyself.com/What_attracts_men_the_ psychology_of_attraction_of_males**, [Accessed: 19/06/19]

Bressert, S. (2018), Female & Male Orgasmic Disorder Symptoms, https://psychcentral.com/disorders/female-male-orgasmic-disorder-symptoms/ [Accessed: 9/07/19]

Psychology Today (2019), Orgasmic Disorder, **https://www.psychologytoday.com/us/conditions/orgasmi c-disorder** [Accessed: 9/07/19]

Muehlenhard, CL, & Kimes, LA (1999), The social construction of violence-The case of sexual & domestic violence, Personal & Social Psychology Rev, 3(3), 234-245

Gullum, T. L. (2009), The Intersection of Spirituality, Religion and Intimate Partner Violence in the African American Community, Available online:
https://www.communitysolutionsva.org/files/TheIntersectionofSpirituali ty%281%29.pdf, [Accessed on 10/01/2019]

Barter, C., McCarry, M., Berridge, D. and Evans, K. (2009) Partner exploitation and violence in teenage intimate relationships. London: NSPCC.

Baskerville, R. F. (2003), Hofstede never studied culture, Accounting, Organizations and Society, pp. 28 1–14

Gov.UK. (2015, January 21), Equality Act 2010: guidance. Retrieved from Gov.UK: https://www.gov.uk/guidance/equality-act-2010-guidance.

Bolton, D. (2008), What is mental disorder? An essay in philosophy, science and values. Oxford: University Press.

Cheng, Q., Hong, L., Silenzio, V., & Caine, E. D. (2014), Suicide Contagion: A Systematic Review of Definitions and Research Utility. Plos One, 9 (9), 1-9

Roger, A., & Pilgrim, D. (2003). Mental Health and Inequality. London: Palgrave Macmillan.

28499972R00069

Printed in Great Britain
by Amazon